A FINE CHAOS

THREE YEARS RENOVATING A CASTLE IN CHILE

DAVID MILLS

ISBN: 978-1-4834-0947-4 (sc)
ISBN: 978-1-4834-0946-7 (e)

Lulu Publishing Services rev. date: 04/16/2014

"The Chilean Andes are a fine chaos of mountains spreading away. They are sublime, like hearing a chorus of the Messiah in full orchestra."

Charles Darwin, 1835

CONTENTS

Prologue...ix

Chapter One: Where is Chile, Anyway? 1

Chapter Two: Castillo Verde... 13

Chapter Three: The Origins of the Potato, Pisco, and Why it
        Takes so Long to Cross the Border.............................. 21

Chapter Four: There Are a Lot of Dogs in Chile.................... 31

Chapter Five: Blood Has Been Spilled Over Water................ 41

Chapter Six: Chile Can be a Bit Bureaucratic....................... 49

Chapter Seven: Diez y Ocho, Septiembre............................... 59

Chapter Eight: Santiago's Yellow Death................................. 73

Chapter Nine: Carlito's Way 87

Chapter Ten: The Noble Chilean Horse 95

Chapter Eleven: I Learn My Brain is Made of Teflon.......... 103

Chapter Twelve: The Carabineros Are Our Friends 113

Chapter Thirteen: The Project Begins 121

Chapter Fourteen: The Second Spanish Invasion 131

Chapter Fifteen: In Vino Veritas 143

Chapter Sixteen: Luis and Roberto 153

Chapter Seventeen: Neruda's Ghost..................................... 163

Chapter Eighteen: What Will the Future Bring? 171

PROLOGUE

March 25, 2005

It was one of those heartbreaking days in late-March when winter returns with a vengeance. We had endured a long and harsh season in the northern hemisphere, damp and deeply cold with frequent ice storms, freezing rain and that fine, misty snow that is anything but picturesque. The steady accumulations of snow for the most part appeared during Sunday nights, requiring pre-dawn Mondays with the shovel to dig out the car before showering, dressing, and then fighting the clogged highways to work with no time for a decent breakfast.

But March had, as the saying goes, arrived like a lamb. Mid-month the sun appeared for several days on end. The snow melted in long meandering rivers down the street as the banks around the house slowly disappeared. The air turned warm, the breeze was fresh, and spring was in the air. The mud of November, so discouraging in what it portends, was transformed into the promise of flowers, ferns and the rest of our garden appearing over the ensuing months. There were a few buds on the trees with occasional snowdrops peeking up from among the mat of moldy leaves. Robins appeared from the south, the true harbinger of spring, gathering twigs and other bits with which to build their nests. Maybe this year March, having arrived like a lamb, would not leave like a lion.

And then the snow returned, accompanied by high winds and sub-zero temperatures, dashing any hopes of an early spring. I was sitting at my desk, despondently peering out through the so familiar swirl and eddies of snow spiraling down from the sky, hoping the robins would not be in trouble as their food and nesting supplies rapidly disappeared under the drifts. Then the telephone rang. It was my wife.

"Hi honey. I love you. I want to buy a house in Chile."

From: dgmills@sympatico.ca
To: alan@concord.ca
Date: March 26, 2005

Dear Alan,

As you may be aware by now, Karen has broached the subject of buying a decrepit, wrecked and ruined shell of a house in South America. You have spent some time with her in Chile and have seen the so-called house she wants us to purchase. I also know that, as one of her best clients and a real friend, you have a lot of influence with her and that your advice is welcome and respected.

I have a proposition for you. If you are able to talk her out of buying this property, I will donate $10,000 in your name to the charity of your choice. Where the hell is Chile, anyway? Is it not one of the most dangerous countries on earth? Is it not consumed with violence, crime, corruption and overrun with soldiers just looking for an excuse to detain, or better, shoot someone? Is not communism rampant, or did I hear correctly that the country is governed by a far right police and military junta for whom human rights is a four-letter word? Has Karen lost her mind?

All the best,
David

From: alan@concord.ca
To: dgmills@sympatico.ca
Date: March 27, 2005

Dear David,

Thanks for your e-mail. While I understand your concern, I really think you need to come down to Chile and see for yourself what the country has to offer. It is quite an amazing place. As for the offer of the payment to a charity, after seeing the house Karen has in mind, I believe you will need every penny you can find.

Besides, we both know full well it is almost impossible to say no to your wife.

Look forward to seeing the finished project.

Alan

From: alan@concord.ca
To: karen.mills@gmail.com
Date: March 27, 2005

Dear Karen,

David has just sent me an e-mail offering to contribute $10,000 to a charity if I talk you out of buying the property in Chile. Wondering what you might counter-offer?

Just kidding,
Alan

CHAPTER ONE

WHERE IS CHILE, ANYWAY?

T he plane was descending into Santiago's Comodoro Arturo Merino Benitez International airport on my first visit to Chile after a ten hour overnight flight from Toronto. Karen and I had slept about five hours, with my wife the more experienced at catching forty winks on an airplane as this was her third trip to South America. I would have slept longer except I was awoken at dawn to watch our progress south as we tracked the spectacular Andes Mountains that divide Chile from its eastern neighbours.

Chile possesses a geological and geographic footprint that is unique in the world. Despite being one of the smallest countries in South America, covering only about 800,000 square kilometers, it extends more than 4,300 kilometres from north to south, almost as long as Canada extends from east to west, but is, on average, only 175 kilometers wide. The landscape climbs dramatically in this short distance from sea level to some of the highest mountain peaks in the world rising well above 7,000 meters.

Bounded by the Pacific Ocean to the west and the Andes to the east, Chile includes the world's driest desert to the north, verdant and lush vineyards and gardens benefiting from a Mediterranean-like climate in the central heart of the country, south through a beautiful lake region that would rival the English countryside or Canada's cottage country, to the sub-Arctic splendor of Patagonia and a large part of Antarctica. Chile also holds dominion over Easter Island (Rapa Nui) and its fabled stone monuments, a four hour flight to the west of the mainland isolated in the middle of the Pacific Ocean.

The country's population numbers approximately 15 million, with almost half living in and around the city of Santiago. About a million Chileans are Mapuche Indians, one of the most out-spoken and proud indigenous populations in all of South America, with the majority of the balance descendants of the original Spanish and English colonists over the past 500 years. Adding to this mix are immigrants from other South American countries seeking employment in Chile's strong economy, as well as Europeans and North Americans, like us, attracted to the country's fabulous climate and stable political environment.

I continue to be surprised that tourists have not discovered Chile in larger numbers. The warm and non-humid Chilean summer, which peaks in the months of January and February, corresponds to the northern hemisphere's coldest and most challenging winter weather. There are cultural and outdoor adventure activities to satisfy the most demanding traveler, and in the Chilean winter months of July and August spectacular skiing can be found within a two-hour drive of Santiago.

With Chile lying in the same eastern seaboard time zone as Washington, New York and Toronto, jet lag is not an issue. And yet in 2005 only two million tourists visited the country, with over 1.2 million of these arriving from other South American countries. Compare this paltry number with the more than twenty million tourists that visited Canada in the same year. Tourism represented only 1.3% of total Chilean Gross Domestic Product in 2005, much lower than the 8% of GDP in Mexico and Costa Rica.

Chile is also not plagued by many dangerous reptiles, insects, sea creatures or plants. I remember Bill Bryson stating in his wonderful book about Australia, "In a Sunburned Country", that of the ten most poisonous creatures on earth, eight lived and thrived in Australia. Fortunately, to our knowledge, none of these are resident in Chile.

There is one small creature, however, that can cause some distress. A species of black widow spider found in the far south of the country – the *latrodectus mactans* – can be fatal to some children and the elderly. However, the spider's venom apparently can also provide some significant benefits to others as, for younger men, a bite can cause prolonged and involuntary erections, sometimes lasting days, and reported superhuman virility. Scientists are studying the spider's venom and have discovered it also contains spermicidal properties that can act as an effective contraceptive as well as a natural antidote for erectile dysfunction. In this case I believe Nietzsche was correct – *that which does not kill us makes us stronger.*

Possibly one of the reasons people are not visiting Chile is a general lack of knowledge about the country and, indeed, all of South America. Certainly I knew very little about the region, and had to dig out my atlas following Karen's March 2005 telephone call to make sure I knew where Chile was located. Most of our friends were also unsure where Chile was, and very few had traveled to the continent.

There is generally little news about the country in the daily media. The inconsequential presence Chile commands on the international stage can be summed up by a competition conducted by the editors of England's famed newspaper, "The Times", for the most factually correct yet most boring headline. The winning headline by a large majority, attributed to the respected journalist and sub-editor Claud Cockburn, was *"Small Earthquake in Chile - Not Many Dead"*.

Another reason for the lack of visitors to the country may derive from the perception that South America in general, and Chile in particular, is not safe. These beliefs are most likely shaped by the turmoil and political unrest Chile experienced over the last forty years.

The opening decade of the twentieth century looked very bright for the country. Its economy was strong, supported by the massive volumes of high quality mineral resources mined in the country's northern regions and exported to markets around the world.

The main product discovered in the North was nitrate, used primarily in the production of fertilizer in the United States, the United Kingdom and Europe. The Atacama Desert, where these valuable resources were discovered, is the driest region on the planet, averaging less than ten millimeters of rainfall annually. Frequently years can go by without any moisture being seen at all. Off the coast of this dry, desert region the cold waters of the Pacific Ocean are home to massive schools of fish that, for millennia, have been the feeding grounds for numerous sea birds such as pelicans, cormorants and gulls. While these birds found their food in the oceans, they lived on the land and, for thousands and thousands of years, deposited their droppings in an area with little rainfall to wash it away. The centuries of guano deposits from these birds formed into piles several meters thick, providing Chile with a highly valuable and unique mineral resource that was in high demand by farmers around the world.

The Atacama Desert and the Chilean economy at the turn of the century also benefited from deposits of other minerals left behind by snow melt running off the high Andes Mountains at the end of the winter. This mineral-laden water formed pools and, under the hot dry sun, quickly evaporated leaving behind another unique mineral product called *caliche*, or saltpeter. It too experienced strong market demand as, with its high concentrations of nitrogen and phosphorous, it became a key ingredient in the production of gunpowder and explosives.

However, in the early years of the twentieth century, the Chilean economy was dealt a series of severe blows, beginning with the invention of synthetic nitrates in Europe that devastated what was the main export for the nation and by far the largest component of its Gross Domestic Product (GDP), or *Producto Interno Bruto (PIB)*. Compounding this disaster was the opening of the Panama Canal in 1914 which significantly reduced the number of ocean-going vessels that previously had been forced to travel around Cape Horn at the globe's southern tip and up the Chilean coast. Then, with the outbreak of the First World War, most trade between Chile and its partners in England and Europe was suspended, further isolating this tiny country at the other end of the world.

As Chile's northern nitrate towns closed, the remaining sectors of the economy, largely agrarian, could not absorb the thousands of displaced and mostly uneducated workers who gradually drifted toward the large cities of Santiago and Valparaiso in search of work. Compounding this move to the city was the state of the country's agricultural industry at that time. The vast majority of farms and agricultural businesses were owned by a very few wealthy landowners who were also contributing to the unprecedented high unemployment levels as they adopted more mechanized farming techniques and reduced their dependence on manual labour.

As a result of the mounting social pressures and economic setbacks arising from these dramatic changes to the social and economic fabric of the country, Chile began to drift politically to the left as successive governments were unable to revive the economy or improve the country's education, health care or working conditions. Eventually more interventionist initiatives were employed through the establishment of state-owned corporations. All of these trends culminated in the election of President Salvador Allende in 1970, the world's first, and so far only, freely-elected Marxist head of state.

Allende faced a daunting task as he tried to redistribute Chile's wealth through constitutional and legislative means. The country was severely polarized along political lines, with both the left and the right despising and mistrusting each other. Adding to this challenging situation was the growing concern in Washington as Richard Nixon, along with his advisor Henry Kissinger, viewed the new socialist government in Chile as a significant threat to South American stability. It didn't help that President Allende was a good friend and vocal supporter of the Cuban revolution and its new leader Fidel Castro.

Among President Allende's first initiatives was to nationalize the Chilean copper industry, previously owned and financed by foreign interests. The government also began to implement a land reform program that contemplated breaking up the vast land holdings owned by what the government viewed as the privileged elite, and redistributing these properties to the people who had worked these lands for generations. Unfortunately for President Allende, his actions enraged the right, while the left did not think he was going far enough or fast enough. Soon the country was plagued by double-digit inflation, and a series of labour strikes that paralyzed its economy.

The end came on September 11, 1973 as the army, under the leadership of General Augusto Pinochet, removed the elected government in a violent coup and installed what would become one of the longest-standing and most repressive military dictatorships the world has ever known. During the pitched battles on September 11, Salvador Allende is reported to have committed suicide in Santiago's La Moneda Presidential Palace with a gun given to him by his friend Fidel Castro.

The Pinochet regime was brutal in quickly taking control of the country. Immediately, and over the next few years, thousands of Allende supporters, and many people who were innocently in the wrong place at the wrong time, were rounded up, tortured and murdered. Called "the disappeared", to this day many families do not know what happened to their loved ones, and probably never will. Political parties were banned, civil liberties suspended, and a curfew that lasted well into the 1980's was enforced requiring people to be off the streets by 11.00 pm. The murderous police state even extended its reach into other countries with the assassination of a Chilean General in Buenos Aires in 1974 and the Chilean diplomat Orlando Letelier with a car bomb in Washington DC in 1976.

The regime also undertook a complete and wide-ranging overhaul of the Chilean economy, inspired in large part by what was known as the "Chicago School", a group of free-market economists from the United States under the direction of Milton Friedman. The state-owned enterprises established by Salvador Allende's government were sold to the private sector, allegedly with many Pinochet supporters getting plum deals. Government and business regulations were significantly eased to attract foreign capital, and private health care and pension plans were implemented to compete with state-run programs. Gradually, and over many years, the Chilean economy diversified and strengthened, mostly due to global demand for the country's abundance of natural resources, and in particular the world's largest deposits of copper.

In 1980 General Pinochet was confident enough that his reforms and, in his perception, economic recovery, had resulted in sufficient good will that he could hold a plebiscite to establish a new constitution and extend his Presidency until 1989. While the plebiscite was confirmed, the majority of citizens either spoiled their ballots or abstained from voting. It was a meaningless victory.

In 1987, again confident of public support, Pinochet began to permit the re-establishment of political parties and to allow more open and, importantly, more public discourse. He also decided to hold another plebiscite to further extend his power until 1997. This time, however, people were emboldened by the laxer enforcement of dissent and spoke out against the regime. The new era of openness culminated on April 25, 1988 in a televised debate in which Richard Lagos, a socialist party leader and future President of the country, pointed his finger at General Pinochet and said: "You promise this country another eight years of torture, disappearances and human rights violations". When Lagos was not arrested for his opposition outburst, the electorate felt safe and Pinochet's plebiscite was defeated by a wide margin.

With this defeat, provisional governments were elected, of course with the dictatorship's permission, in 1989 and again in 1993. However, most of the power and influence over politics and the economy, under a constitution written and implemented by the Pinochet regime, remained with the military dictatorship.

The tide turned in October 1998 when Scotland Yard officially arrested General Pinochet during his visit to London, England for back surgery. The arrest was made for alleged violations of human rights on behalf of a Spanish judge investigating the deaths and disappearance of several of his country's citizens in Chile during the early period of the Pinochet regime. After two years of judicial wrangling, and the refusal of the Chilean government, still under military control, to support any trial procedures outside of the country, Pinochet was allowed to return to Chile in March 2000 on the grounds of ill health, where he immediately underwent house arrest. On December 11, 2006 he died in the Santiago Military Hospital of natural causes after the Chilean nation endured almost seven years wondering whether or not he would be brought to trial and answer for his crimes.

It is difficult to talk to Chileans about their views of this troubled period in their history, and it is obviously a very tender subject. Those who supported the General's regime are normally quiet and restrained in their opinions given the world's condemnation of his alleged human rights abuses, and that fact that so many benefited economically during and after his reforms. Those who opposed the military rule are also quiet as they wait for some form of justice to play out in the courts for what happened to them and their families. The most vocal are the Mothers of the "disappeared", who publicly mourn the loss of their children and continually demand answers by parading in front of military headquarters across the country with placards bearing pictures of their missing loved ones.

General Pinochet's funeral was a real insight into how the Chilean people are dealing with their recent past. In a move to placate both sides of the issue, and in a spirit of true compromise, the government did not allow a full state funeral for the General, but did permit the armed forces to hold their own elaborate ceremony. No politicians attended the funeral, except for the Minister of Defence, who represented the government in keeping with that office. The funeral and ceremonies were televised, and no one appeared offended.

We were in Chile on the day the General passed away, and there were demonstrations throughout the country by both his supporters and his opponents. It was fascinating to see, and try to understand, what this man meant to the people of Chile. For some, he was their saviour, and thousands gathered outside the hospital, in town squares, parks, restaurants, bars and homes to mourn his passing. For others, Pinochet stood next to Satan in terms of personifying evil, and they danced jubilantly in the streets long into the night. And for some, it was simply an excuse to riot.

A certain "loutish" element in Chile just loves to run around, yell, burn cars and tires, set up barricades, throw things at police, disrupt everyday lives, and generally misbehave. In turn, the police and the military believe they must respond, and when these demonstrations occur, out come their own gates and barricades, the water cannons, and the lines of truncheon wielding, plastic shielded and helmeted police. On the day of the General's death, things were complicated as one of the country's major soccer teams, Colo Colo, had that same afternoon won a major match, and thousands of the team's supporters were already in the streets, well lubricated from wine, beer and the ever-present pisco, looking for something to do. Pinochet's death was just the spark, and off they went.

Watching on television, the demonstrations seemed harmless enough – a bit like a big chess match, really. I do not want to make light of the events of that day, and I have since learned that there were some serious injuries and numerous arrests during the riots, but there appeared to be a highly practiced ebb and flow to the demonstrations that seemed almost choreographed. The unruly crowd would advance on the barricades set up by the authorities and perhaps throw a few rocks or overturn a fence or two. Then in would come the police with their water cannons to hose them down and send them running for shelter. Occasionally tear gas might be directed toward the crowd. In response, one or two crazies from the retreating demonstrators would hurl the tear gas canisters back at the police, or stand, arms raised in supplication, in front of the powerful water cannon jets. And then it would start all over again. The demonstrations went on for hours until, I suppose, everyone got tired and went home.

As I learn more and more about Chile's recent history, I increasingly recognize that I will never truly understand what this country and its people have gone through. During the time average Chileans were being taken from their homes, savagely beaten, tortured and murdered, I was calmly attending a large University in Toronto. My generation in Canada is privileged as, in large part, we have not experienced a war, gone through a cataclysmic social or environmental disaster, or experienced, other than in the natural course of things, death. While Chileans my age were heroically opposing a repressive regime and trying just to stay alive, my priorities were to learn how to drink alcohol, smoke pot, listen to music, read obscure literary and philosophical texts, and then find a first job in a booming economy, settle down and start a family.

One evening, a new-found Chilean friend was telling us about his period of incarceration in a Pinochet prison camp. He had been arrested because he had been a vocal supporter of the Allende government and had been held, along with more than 2,000 other detainees, in an institution designed to only hold 200 people. Despite the obvious hardship and despair he must have endured for the three months he lived in these overcrowded and squalid conditions, the first story he related to us demonstrated, for him, the wonderful spirit and sense of humour his fellow prisoners displayed.

Apparently, two brothers, peasant farmers from the region, had been arrested on suspicion of hiding guns and ammunition for the communist rebels. In reality, they may have owned one or two rifles used to deter predators from their lands, and were not involved in any larger conspiracy. Nevertheless, the soldiers beat them with clubs over a number of hours, in full view of all the prisoners, demanding to know where they had hidden their forbidden cache of arms. Upon repeated denials by the prisoners, the interrogators changed their tact and, with further beatings, ordered them to reveal the whereabouts of a truck they allegedly used to transport opposition troops and arms. The brothers were equally mystified by this charge and professed to know nothing about the existence of any such truck or any such conspiracy.

The soldiers took a break, and then brought the brothers back in front of the prisoners to re-start the interrogation. With their clubs raised, they once again demanded to know the location of the hidden guns and ammunition. On bended knee, bleeding and bruised from the previous beatings, one brother looked at the other and answered: "I guess they are in the truck". Everyone in the prison yard collectively held their breath, and then, one by one, began to laugh.

So will I ever be able to understand what Chile and its people have gone through? I won't, and I never will. But I do see, and can appreciate, the dignity of the Chilean people and the healing that is occurring as its citizens try, and for the most part succeed, to put their anger, their rage and their thirst for revenge behind them to move their country, their culture and their society, forward. I cannot imagine what they must feel, but I can admire and respect the strength it takes for them to do this in a positive way.

This is also a country that reveres and points to its heroes, not the usual sports figures, Hollywood celebrities, gun-totting soldiers or smiling politicians, but rather two Nobel-prize winning poets – Gabriela Mistral in 1945 and Pablo Neruda in 1971. It is a country with one of the world's largest per capita Catholic populations, a nation that only legalized divorce in 2004, and one that still operates under the strange Latin code of machismo where women are whistled at as they walk down the street. And yet it surprises the world by electing an acknowledged agnostic and twice-divorced woman for a six-year term as President, a person whose father died after being tortured by the Pinochet regime and who was herself jailed, mistreated and forced into exile. Yes, this is a country and a people that I want to get to know.

But on this first trip to Chile, I did not come to understand its people, their culture, or their politics, but to buy one of their houses.

CHAPTER TWO
CASTILLO VERDE

T he genesis of our adventure in Chile began with my wife, Karen, who had first come to the country in 2004 to work with the celebrated Chilean sculptor Francisco Gazitua.

Señor Gazitua, known as Pancho to his friends, is one of South America's most prestigious and award-winning visual artists. Born in Santiago in 1944, he works in wood, stone and forged steel to create large works destined for public spaces, as well as smaller, more personal pieces that are treasured by private collectors and museums around the world. He studied philosophy and sculpture in Chile, and completed a postgraduate degree at St. Martin's School of the Arts in London, England. He has taught sculpture for thirty-five years in Chile and England, as well as in the United States, Europe and Brazil, and he continues to work with students in his studio situated in the foothills of the central Andes Mountains. His larger scale works are situated throughout Santiago and other major cities in Chile, as well as in Canada, England, Bolivia, the U.S., Portugal, Lebanon, Costa Rica, Mexico and Sweden. In 2007 he was made a Member of the prestigious Belgian Royal Academy in recognition of his contribution to the art of sculpture.

Pancho's inspiration for his work is derived from the oceans and the ships that ply its waves, the mountains that surround his home, the trees he sees on his treks throughout Chile, and the horses on which he takes these journeys. The natural elements in which he lives, and the environment he values so much, are central to his work and inform all that he does. He has created large, boat-like sculptures and massive horses in forged steel, as well as more conceptual works in wood and stone inspired by these themes. His compelling public art commissions draw on the poetry and history of each specific site to create a strong relationship between the artwork, its location, and the viewer. Pancho does extensive research into the history of each location where his sculptures will be located, and creatively weaves the key elements of this history into his works.

On meeting Pancho for the first time, you are struck by his integrity, his strength of character, and his youthfulness. You also cannot avoid his joy of life, his desire to be and to do the best, and his wonderful sense of humour. He loves to laugh, and his embracing of life is completely infectious. One can't help but be intrigued and intellectually challenged in his company, and the times we have spent together have been a true joy.

Pancho's wife, Angela Lieble, is also a celebrated artist. Born in Santiago and with degrees in geology and painting, Angela has held numerous important exhibitions of her work in major galleries in Santiago and Buenos Aires, Argentina. An accomplished rider, her large-scale paintings depict the Chilean horse at work and at rest, and include as her subjects only those animals she has personally raised, trained and groomed, her companions on the many trips she has taken with Pancho into the heart of the Andes. Focusing on the animal's skeleton and musculature, her works present a dynamic and powerful view of the horse and rider as they perform their daily routines of tracking, working livestock in the mountains, or exploring.

Angela too is wonderful company, although if I were to look for one adjective to describe her, it would be fierce. While of Italian and German descent, she clearly has native Andean blood in her and is a descendant of an Inca Chief. Her piercing gaze, her aquiline but extremely attractive profile, and her often intemperate tongue can be a bit intimidating at times, yet her laugh, and her ability to welcome you into her home and her life, quickly make you feel comfortable as though she had known you for years.

In 2004 Pancho had won an international competition to install a commissioned sculpture in the middle of a large condominium project in downtown Toronto being built by Concord Adex, one of the world's premier real estate developers. My wife Karen was responsible for managing the entire process, from the initial design and concept of the artwork through its construction, shipment to Canada, and its installation on site. As Pancho was fabricating the entire sculpture at his mountainside studio outside Santiago, Karen was required to make periodic visits to monitor its progress, along with her client's engineers, landscape architects and senior executives.

As Pancho did not have the space to host what could be as many as five to ten visitors at a time, he approached his good friends the Letelier family who owned a large home nearby – *Casa Blanca*. Jorge Letelier, Casa Blanca's owner, was spending most of his time in New York City furthering his career as one of the world's leading interior designers. It was left to his sister Marcela and her husband Sergio to look after Karen and the other Canadian guests.

Casa Blanca is a beautiful, spacious estancia surrounded by well-kept flower and native plant gardens situated on a bluff overlooking the Maipo River in the town of San Juan de Pirque, approximately 40 kilometers south and east of Santiago. Situated in the steep foothills of the Andes Mountains, the property is encircled by spectacular views of snow-capped peaks, the river valley, and lush vineyards and orchards of various fruit and almond trees. Marcela and Sergio, as well as Pancho and Angela, were the best hosts for Karen and her guests, and everyone in her group was included in their hosts' social plans, parties, trips to wine country and the seaside, and many other adventures.

It was late March 2005, and the Chilean phase of Pancho's sculpture project had begun to wind down. The Letelier's, who had become good friends with Karen though the many weeks she had spent with them, mentioned that they would like to remain in touch, meet her husband and family and, wouldn't you know, the property next door – *Castillo Verde*, or the Green Castle - was for sale. Cleverly, the pitch to become neighbours was made after a very long lunch at which much wine was consumed.

Karen and our daughter Sarah, who was also visiting Chile at that time to plan a documentary film about Pancho's Toronto installation, walked next door to view the property. It was then I received that fateful telephone call as I was sitting at my desk in Canada, glumly staring out at the return of winter.

Roughly two weeks later Karen and I returned to Chile to explore the house and property and, perhaps, meet the owner to discuss a potential purchase.

Castillo Verde, originally built in the early 1930's, had essentially been abandoned for five years by the current owner. It was a two-storey house constructed of large granite blocks with a slate roof and a charming ivy-covered, castle-like turret acting as its front door - hence the name, *Castillo Verde*. Inside, a leaking roof had caused considerable damage to the wide plank floors and a number of interior walls. The rooms were mostly small and dark, divided by dank hallways, with ivy growing into much of the house through broken windows. The kitchen was narrow and very outdated, and it was clear that neither the electrical or the plumbing systems had been updated in decades. Outside the turret door was a small, oval-shaped swimming pool, empty of water and full of leaves and debris. We had little confidence it would hold water much less operate properly.

The house was perched directly on the edge of a steep and extended cliff that ran down to a narrow local road and then into the Maipo River. The views north and west to the river valley and the glow of Santiago were spectacular, and we immediately realized that the sound of the river flowing over its rock bed would serve as a welcome and restful sound to lull us to sleep. More importantly, the Castillo's exposure to the river valley benefited from a constant and steady light breeze, which the locals call *el raco,* that we knew would cool the property on even the hottest days of the Chilean summer.

At the driveway entrance, accessed through graffiti-covered double steel doors, there was a small three-room adobe house in which lived the property's caretaker, Luis Veloso. This building was also in extremely bad shape, and poor Luis was living with no heat, very little light, and a minimal level of services.

The Castillo was surrounded by what had once been a beautiful and extensive 4,500 square meter garden (about one acre) that for years had been allowed to run rampant. We counted orange, lemon, lime and avocado trees on the property, as well as one of the largest fig trees anyone had ever seen. It was a paradise lost, but as avid gardeners, we knew the bones were there to enable a wonderful transformation.

The property also included a large and untamed hillside of another approximately 4,500 square meters stretching out to the east and below the main table land on which the Castillo was situated. There was a rudimentary dirt path that wound down this hill, with a ruined cottage, storage shed and other structures at the bottom. The hill was covered in overgrown almond trees, beautiful Chilean palms, and a large number of flowering plants, all of which were choked by weeds and debris, dead leaves, and copious amounts of bark shed by the numerous eucalyptus trees that towered over and shaded the hillside property. It was a mess.

But again, as we explored the hillside and land below, it became clear that at one time this too had been a well cared for and loved garden. There were overgrown footpaths that took different routes up the hill, with small terraces at various vantage points offering views of the river and its surrounding countryside. There were rusty pipes and seized taps that once had been used to water the entire hillside, and a number of stone walls, now crumbling and falling down, defined garden borders and the paths the someone in the past had used to traverse their land. It clearly had been an extremely exotic and extensive garden, and we believed it could be again.

As we finished our tour of Castillo Verde and its surrounding property, Karen and I looked at each other with the same question in our minds. We had recently completed one major house and garden restoration in Canada – as we moved into our mid-50's, did we want to tackle another, more challenging renovation over 5,000 miles away in a foreign country and in a language neither of us spoke? We decided to take the next step and meet the owner.

Carlos was an architect by trade who, on the untimely death of his first wife, had moved out of Castillo Verde with his children to live further up the mountain and build a new life tending a grove of almond trees. He had been trying to sell Castillo Verde for more than four years, and had even entertained but rejected an offer from the Leteliers. As a result, we had a decent idea of what he wanted for the property, an amount we deemed to be fair based on what we had seen and our initial thoughts on what we would need to invest to make the property habitable again.

Marcela organized the meeting at Casa Blanca in the early evening of a dark and chilly April day, the beginning of fall in Chile. We were told that meetings such as this could last some time as it was customary to share some wine and socializing before getting down to business. When Carlos arrived, we talked about our families, our businesses, our activities, and our lives both in Chile and in Canada. After a couple of hours, it became clear it was time to move on to the matter at hand.

Carlos opened the discussion by saying that he was not going to sell the property to just anyone. Castillo Verde, he informed us, had been built by the late Victoria Mackenna, who, with her husband, owned the substantial Parque Mackenna in which the house was originally situated. The Castillo had been designed and constructed by Mrs. Mackenna for her lover, and was therefore, as Carlos told us, "a house built on love". Any new owner must understand this, take care of the property, and love it as much as he and his family had. In fact, he said, he must feel "*simpatico*" with anyone to whom he would sell the property.

Without asking why someone who loved a property so much could allow it to descend into such ruin, I pulled out my business card and handed it to him. My e-mail address at that time used a well-known Canadian web hosting service called Sympatico, and my address included this word as its domain name. As I handed the card to him, I told him that we certainly understood the concept of "*simpatico*" and pointed to my e-mail address.

He appeared dumfounded and examined the card closely. After a few moments, he looked up with a big smile and said: "Perfecto. I sell my house to you".

We then underwent an extended hour or so of price negotiations, with each offer and counter offer being met by demonstrations of dismay, disappointment, hand wringing and disbelief. Finally, we agreed on a price that was half way between what he wanted to receive and what we wanted to pay. We shook hands, and that was that.

Or so we thought. Little did we know it would be almost sixteen months before we actually got the keys and could call Castillo Verde our own.

CHAPTER THREE

THE ORIGINS OF THE POTATO, PISCO, AND WHY IT TAKES SO LONG TO CROSS THE BORDER

Despite its relative isolation on the world stage, Chile is not without issues with its neighbour Argentina to the east, and Peru and Bolivia to the North.

The troubles initially began in the mid-nineteenth century over disputes as to who controlled the rich mineral deposits of nitrate and *caliche* in the Atacama Desert. Borders in the region at the turn of the century were a bit vague, and as Chile, with the aid primarily of British interests, initially began exploiting the vast resources, neighbouring Bolivia and Peru wanted to participate and cash in on the wealth being created.

As the Chilean economy began to worsen through the late-1800's and exports declined, the country's foreign debt began to increase steadily, nearly doubling in the ten years leading up to 1870. Chile began looking more covetously at the Atacama and its mineral resources, and decided to take full control of the region. In its defence, most of the extraction and export work was being done by Chilean companies and their workers, and the government felt justified in claiming the lands as their own.

The straw that broke the back of the dispute was a move by Bolivia to impose a tax on all exports from the region. Despite the fact that the monies levied by the tax were going to be used to enhance the coastal port of Antofagasta, from where all of the valuable resources were exported, Chile decided to assert its claim, put together an army and declared war on Bolivia and Peru in 1879. Chile then quickly sent a warship to the port city of Antofagasta, landed 2,000 soldiers, and claimed the city without a fight. At the same time Chile ensured Argentina would remain on the sidelines as, although its easterly neighbour had defense treaties with both Bolivia and Peru, it was also contesting its border with Chile in Patagonia, and did not want to cause problems in these negotiations.

Thus began the War of the Pacific, fought on both the sea and on land for approximately five years, resulting in Chile annexing the Peruvian provinces of Tarapaca and Arica and the Bolivian province of Litoral, in effect the entire Atacama Desert region. The loss of the war deprived Peru of valuable minerals and territory, and shut off any access by Bolivia to the ocean, effectively landlocking the country.

To this day Chile's victory still rankles in both defeated countries, and political relations remain strained with Chile. Numerous overtures by Bolivia to gain access to the ocean have been rebuffed, and the country continues to suffer economically from a lack of ability to efficiently export its abundant natural resources. A week does not go by in Bolivia without a newspaper editorial on the subject, and the general population continues to blame their poor economic performance on Chile. It is both an emotional and practical issue for both Bolivians and Chileans.

In recent decades each successive Bolivian President has made it government policy to pressure Chile for access to the sea. And there have been quite a few Bolivian Presidents, given the country's propensity for revolution. The Guinness Book of Records claims that Bolivia has had more coups d'état than any other country in recorded history. There have been 187 coups since its independence in 1825, causing many to refer to the country as a "long-playing record – thirty-three revolutions per minute". As an aside, Queen Victoria, so enraged that the British foreign minister had been expelled during one coup strapped to the back of a donkey, ordered Bolivia to be removed from all world maps produced in Great Britain.

But the lingering issues from the war of the Pacific pale in comparison to the question of who invented pisco, and who first discovered the potato.

Experts agree that the humble potato, a staple in diets around the world, has its origins in South America. The potato is the world's most widely grown tuber crop, and the fourth largest food crop after rice, wheat and corn. The claim to which country is home to this popular vegetable came to a head in 2008, the United Nation's *Year of the Potato*.

In preparing to celebrate the tuber's heritage, the UN stated that the first wild potato plants were cultivated near Lake Titicaca in southern Peru round 7,000 years ago. Chile disputed this fact, with the country's Minister of Agriculture boldly claiming DNA tests have shown that almost all of the 7,000 varieties of potato grown around the world are derived from plants grown on Chile's Chiloe Island. National pride in both countries became inflamed, with Peruvian editorials and the government accusing the Chileans of trying to usurp yet another national achievement, and of course bringing the War of the Pacific into the fray as a further example of the Chilean invasion of all things sacred in Peru.

Finally the scientists passed on their exhaustive studies, indicating that, in fact, both countries were correct. Their research indicated that, while it is true approximately three-quarters of potato varieties grown outside of South America are derived from Chile's native spud, it was also true that this version was a grandchild of Peru's original *solanum tuberosum*, a variety not found outside the country. So who won? As in all things South American, no one wins, all sides of the dispute are a little bit right, everyone clams a victory, and everyone is a little bit upset.

Another, and perhaps more long-lasting dispute to arise following the War of the Pacific, was the claim to one of South America's most popular libations, *pisco*. A brandy-like liquor distilled from grapes, *pisco's* origins are widely regarded as dating from the early 1600's in Peru. The drink, first made by farmers from grapes discarded as not suitable for wine production by their Spanish conquerors, became popular with sailors who called it *pisco* after the name of the port city on the south coast of Peru where it could be obtained. It quickly became the liquor of choice for sailors plying South America's trade routes, and by the beginning of the 17th century it almost equaled wine in volume as a Peruvian export.

Unfortunately for Peru, the bulk of Pico production was derived from the Tarapaca region, a province that Chile annexed following their victory in the 1883 War of the Pacific. Over the following century, production of pisco in this new Chilean territory increased significantly to where the country now produces more than fifty times more *pisco* by volume than Peru. To make matters worse, in the 1960's Chile banned the import of any product from Peru that called itself *pisco*. In retaliation, Peru has tried to enforce on world markets the denomination of *pisco* as a Peruvian-only product, and has applied to internationally register the name and its country of origin with the World Intellectual Property Organization. I don't think the dispute over the origins of *pisco* will lead to another armed conflict, but if you want to inflame the rhetoric of a native from either Peru or Chile, all you need to do is comment that the other county's *pisco* is superior and then stand back.

In Chile there are four grades of *pisco*: Regular (30% to 35% alcohol by content), Special (35% to 40%), Reserve (40% to 43%) and Great (43% or higher). Most grades are slightly yellow in colour owing to their wood aging process - the darker the colour, the longer the aging. Many drink pisco straight, almost as a cognac, but most first encounter the liquor in the popular *pisco sour*. Not a day will go by when you are not offered a glass of this popular aperitif. At any restaurant meal, when you check into a hotel, visit a home or attend an event – *pisco sours* will be served.

The traditional *pisco sour* is made by combining four parts *pisco* with one part each of lemon or lime juice and sugar syrup. Shaken with some egg white and ice, it is normally served very cold in a small fluted glass, similar to a champagne flute. Opinions vary as to the exact combination of these ingredients, the type of lemon or lime used, and whether or not angostura bitters should be added. Chileans take pride in their own particular recipes, and all have their favorite recipes and restaurants that serve *pisco*. Our eldest son has adapted the pisco sour to his own taste, adding one part orange juice to the mix of lemon, resulting in another unique version of this wonderful aperitif.

Even the derivation of the *pisco sour* is disputed between Chile and Peru. The Chileans claim the drink was invented by a steward from an English ship who, setting up a bar in the northern Chilean town of Iquique, introduced a new drink combining *pisco* with the *limon de pica*, a small lime grown in the area. Peru, however, claims that the popular drink was invented in the early 1920's at the *Bar Morris* in *Jiron de al Union*, Peru. There are apparently quite distinct differences between Peruvian *pisco* and that produced in Chile, and debates can extend long into the night over the relative merits of each country's *pisco sour*.

While the origins of disputes between Chile and its northern neighbours Peru and Bolivia can be easily ascertained, the reasons for Chile's often challenging relationship with Argentina to the east are more difficult to pin down. Both countries seem to dislike one other, and citizens from each look down disdainfully and disparagingly on those of the other as unsophisticated, ill-educated, unattractive and unnecessarily arrogant. I am not sure where these sentiments come from, but they are widely held and prevalent in both countries. And no where else are these feelings displayed so strongly than when you try to enter either country at one of their border crossings.

Mendoza, a beautiful Argentinean wine region located just across the Andes to the east of Santiago, is accessed by a stunning drive through the mountains. Highway 60, running east from Los Andes, a small city about 30 minutes north of Santiago, is well maintained and, although often rising in a series of steep switchbacks up and down some very vertical terrain, is reasonably safe. The most spectacular views can be found as one approaches Portillo, Chile's most famous winter ski resort, and the frequent sightings of Aconcagua, at almost 7,000 meters one of the highest mountains in South America. The route was originally discovered by Pedro de Valdivia as he and his troops first travelled from Argentina through the Andes to conquer the Spanish in Chile, and is the route Charles Darwin took when he first explored Chile and Argentina. The trip is quite arduous by car, and I cannot imagine the hardship these men endured trying to find their way through the maze of passes as they followed the Tupungato River to its source and then over the steep and rugged mountains into Chile. The road twists and winds its way, frequently through a series of tunnels carved into the mountains, and alongside what appears to be an abandoned railway in many places buried under avalanches of rock and debris.

At the summit of the highway driving east toward Argentina, you enter the first of two border patrol crossings. My friend Ian and I were driving to Mendoza to meet up with some friends visiting Argentina, and had been warned that the border crossing could take some time. The first checkpoint was an unexpected pleasure and a surprise as the guard made a cursory inspection of our passports and vehicle documents, provided us with a number of bits of paper with unreadable stamps and scribblings, and sent us on our way. We wondered what all the fuss was about. And then we arrived at the real border crossing.

Greeting us as we rounded a turn in the highway was a massive garage-like structure on the side of the road with a huge parking lot in front. Hundreds of cars, trucks and buses were parked in lines, all pointed toward one single and solitary entrance into the building. Every so often a vehicle would exit at the other end. We were instructed to pull up in a designated line, and then began the wait.

It was simply astonishing how long it took to move toward the building. We turned off our engine, expecting to wait a few minutes before we could move ahead. Thirty minutes later, we had not progressed one inch. Everyone left their cars and walked around, enjoying a snack or lunch, talking with strangers, visiting the restaurant or gift shop, smoking a cigarette, flirting with the opposite sex. Suddenly, everyone would rush back to their vehicles as a few cars exited through the other side of the customs control building and try to jump ahead of any poor hapless sap who might be caught unawares and lose his place in line. Armed soldiers paraded up and down, eying each of us as potential smugglers or terrorists.

Ian and I wondered what could possibly be going on in the customs shed that would take that length of time. Were they strip searching every visitor, dismantling their cars and going through every piece of luggage? We nervously wondered if we had all the necessary documents and if our lack of Spanish would prove an issue. Maybe something momentous had occurred in one or the other country? Had Osama Bin Laden been captured trying to enter Argentina? Perhaps a President had been detained on corruption charges? Had a revolution occurred or a government been overthrown? Could a war have been declared? We had no idea, but it took forever for any vehicle to first enter, and then exit the customs structure.

Ever so slowly we inched our way forward until finally, after almost three hours waiting in line, we entered the building. We then discovered that there were three separate booths we needed to pass. The first examined our personal documents, and this procedure appeared to go fairly well. We tried to answer the questions posed to us in rapidly-spoken Spanish, and discovered that by pointing ahead with our fingers and saying Mendoza over and over again, we seemed to satisfy the first customs guard.

This tactic was not so successful at the second booth. For some reason, this guard was more interested in our car as he tried to ensure, we guessed, that we actually owned our vehicle and that it had all the necessary papers up to date. He wanted to see a number of licenses and official documents that we had no idea if we had in our possession. Finally, I simply handed him everything that was contained in our vehicle's glove compartment, including receipts for gas, chocolate bar wrappers, maps and anything else I could find. I then shrugged, admitting I was an idiot and a gringo, and demonstrated that he should simply search for whatever he needed among the pile of documents. He rifled through everything, and then showed me a sample of some document we did not appear to possess.

We then decided to try our previously successful tactic of pointing ahead and saying Mendoza a few times. We must have worn him down because he finally grimaced in disgust, handed us back our sheaf of papers, added a bunch more official looking documents to the pile, and indicated we were to proceed to the next booth a few meters down the line. This new guard then asked for all of the papers we had just been given by his colleague, stamped them a few more times and made a few additional indecipherable notes, kept a few, gave us a few more, and, after listening and watching us point ahead and say Mendoza a few times, he sent us on our way.

Finally, after more than four hours, we emerged into the sunlight of Argentina and were driving down to meet our friends.

The return back into Chile took almost as long to cross into Argentina and was equally confusing. Chile, like Argentina, is obsessive about protecting their agricultural products, and will not allow any kind of seed, plant, fruit, vegetable, meat or almost any foodstuff into the country from abroad. When you arrive at Santiago's International Airport, and after you clear their passport control, you then have to collect your luggage, fill in another form declaring you have no agricultural products, and then have you and your bags screened by the *Servicio Agricola y Ganadero* (SAG) before you can leave the airport. If you are bringing your pet into the country, they can detain your dog or cat for up to two months in quarantine to make sure they are not bringing any diseases into the country. And while you are waiting for your luggage to appear on the carousel, cute little beagles, setters and golden retrievers wearing tiny green coats with official emblems are sniffing you and your bags for illicit vegetables or fruit.

During our crossing from Mendoza Argentina back into Chile, once again the Chilean border guards appeared more interested in our car than who we were, where we came from, where we were going, or what we might be carrying with us. The vehicle's licenses and documents attracted the most attention and scrutiny, and our tactic of pointing ahead and saying Santiago over and over had little impact with the Chilean border patrols. They also had us fill in the customary forms relating to the importation of agricultural products. As a new Chilean, however, I can say that the Chilean guards seemed more sophisticated, educated, attractive and less arrogant than their Argentinean counterparts.

CHAPTER FOUR

THERE ARE A LOT OF DOGS IN CHILE

e had been staying with Marcela and Sergio at Casa Blanca on our first few visits to Chile, but with their frequent trips to visit friends, their imminent departure for Europe that fall to avoid the Chilean winter, and Jorge remaining in New York, we moved our base of operations to a lovely small cabin, called a *casita*, perched above Pancho and Angela's house on the side of a steep mountain. It was an idyllic space with majestic views to the east over the mountains and the Maipo Valley. The *casita* consisted of a single room with two large and comfortable beds, one of Pancho's signature stone tables, a wood burning stove he had designed and built, a small kitchenette, and a bathroom. As a bonus, the family swimming pool and patio was attached to the casita and we were very fortunate to have this space mostly for our own use.

Pancho and Angela were the best hosts one can imagine, and were too kind to let us use the *casita* essentially as our true home-away-from-home for the next two years. We could come and go as we pleased, and used the *casita* as storage for many of the household items we acquired in Chile or brought from Canada. It quickly began to resemble a refugee camp with boxes and suitcases everywhere.

At night, as the sun set behind us and the mountain peaks glowed in front of us with stunning hues of pink and yellow, we snuggled into our bed under a thick quilt and listened to the dogs begin their all-night ritual of exuberant barking. There are a lot of dogs in Chile.

Pancho says that, when he visits another city or stays in Santiago, he has trouble falling asleep because he does not hear the cacophony of barking dogs to which he has become accustomed in his more rural home. While during the day dogs seem to be lulled to sleep by the sun and the heat, it is once the sun has gone down and night brings the much cooler temperatures that they come to life.

Dogs are a way of life for Chileans. Most own two or three, especially in the countryside where they act as companions and an inexpensive and highly effective security system. These animals are generally not tied up or confined in any way, and are free to roam their neighbourhoods during the night looking for fun and frolic, returning home for meals and sleep during the day.

Adding to their numbers are the vast quantity of *quiltros*, dogs taken into the country and abandoned by their owners. There is one quite remote road running out of Pirque and up the river valley that seems to have become a favorite dumping ground for those not wanting their dogs. The road is populated with many of these animals, so many that some kind soul in the area has taken to buying large sacks of dog food and placing them ripped open on the road side to make sure the strays are fed. They have also posted numerous signs asking people to please not abandon their dogs here, or anywhere.

You see these *quiltros* everywhere in Chile. The cities and towns are full of them – everything from large breeds such as German Shepherds down to the smallest spaniels and beagles, as well as everything in between as they tend to breed indiscriminately. Restaurants are a destination of choice as most Chileans take their meals outside and the *quiltros*, understanding politeness and manners, wait for handouts or sympathetic restaurant owners to feed them.

Another group has purchased a van and, with support from donations, travels the countryside catching these dogs to spay or neuter them. They call their service, appropriately, *"Catch, Cut and Release"*.

Those who are trying to take care of the *quiltros* in our area also visit restaurants and butchers to obtain surplus bones and meat, depositing this welcome source of nourishment along the roadsides for the *quiltros'* well being. On one of my first bicycle rides in the country, I was quite alarmed when I came across a pack of these large, unkempt and wild-looking dogs gnawing on large bloody chunks of meat and bone. Fearing these might be the remains of the last cyclist who had the misfortune to run this gauntlet, I turned and beat a measured but hasty retreat. I learned later that it is very rare for these dogs to harm any human, but it was a bit alarming nevertheless.

Thus, when all the abandoned quiltros come to life in the nighttime, combined with the numerous domesticated pets roaming the forests and fields looking for fun, the concept of exponential growth is well demonstrated. One or two dogs will bark at something, which causes an ever-increasing crescendo of noise to echo through the valley. It is quite humorous, quite loud, and it goes on all night, every night. There really are a lot of dogs in Chile.

At Castillo Verde, the travails of dog ownership became quite apparent. When we first acquired the property, Luis, the caretaker, had one or two dogs living with him. The number seemed to vary whenever we visited. Pancho then gave us two of his Patagonian sheepdog puppies, a beautiful and very noble breed of dog treasured for their intelligence, agility and loyalty. We named the female *Canada* and the male *Canado*, using the correct Spanish language gender format, in honour of our northern home. Unfortunately, one became quite sick and died, while the other, we believe, was spirited away by one of the workers on the renovation project. We then acquired Lazaro, another sheepdog, who then met and brought home a *quiltro* we adopted and named Conejo, the rabbit. Bobby, another quiltro, appeared from somewhere as a puppy, and then our trusted cab driver, Don Alejandro, asked if we could take care of his dog, Valto, who had outgrown their tiny apartment. Ironically, Valto was named after a famous cartoon dog originating in Canada. Soon, Conejo returned to his wanderings and did not return, and Bobby contracted a tumor and died. Today, Lazaro appears infrequently for food and rest after days and sometimes weeks traveling the hinterland, while Valto remains close to home. Whenever we return to Castillo Verde, we glance around to see if our dog population has increased or contracted. It is a normal occurrence in Chile.

Because the dog population in the country is so large, the practice of veterinary medicine has become quite widespread and lucrative. Vets will come to your home to treat your pets, bringing with them any shots, pills or minor surgery that might be required. They will also take your dog away for serious work, such as spaying or neutering, returning the pet to you once it has fully recovered. You can't get this type of home visit from a doctor, but for your dog anything goes.

On our second trip, after reaching a deal on the price for Castillo Verde with Carlos, we arranged to meet with our lawyer, Andres, a partner with Claro y Cia, one of the country's largest legal firms. Marcela kindly loaned us the keys to their charming condo in downtown Santiago as rush hour traffic in and out of the city can be very challenging. We also had no idea where anything was located, or where we were going.

Our ignorance of the city was made most apparent on the morning we were to meet Andres at his office. I awoke early and ventured out into the lovely fresh morning air to find some breakfast – maybe a Starbucks coffee or a Tim Horton's muffin. But as I soon learned, Chileans are not really early-morning people. It was about 7.30 am, yet nothing was open – the cafes, restaurants, newsstands – all were closed and locked.

Apparently the typical workday for the Santiago resident begins around 9.30 or 10.00 in the morning. Stores and shopping malls generally do not open until 11.00 am. Lunch is taken around 1.00 or 2.00 in the afternoon, with many returning home for a little rest, or siesta. They then work until about 7.00 or 8.00 in the evening, with most having their evening meal at the earliest around 10.00 pm. I recall finishing a wonderful dinner at 11.30 pm at an outdoor restaurant in the city centre when two families arrived, both with babies in strollers, to begin their evening meal. No wonder the workday begins at 10.00 in the morning.

Chileans also often enjoy a mid-afternoon meal called *onces*. Consisting of tea and coffee, cakes and sandwiches, it is reminiscent of an English high tea and can serve to tide one over between a lunch and late evening dinner. The name for this repast is derived from a religious order of monks who would leave their prayers in the afternoon to enjoy a glass or two of a local brandy called *aguardiente*. To disguise this frowned-upon pursuit from their elders, they referred to the practice by the number of letters in the name of the spirit – *onces*, Spanish for eleven.

Returning to the condo that first day in Santiago after a fruitless search for a takeaway breakfast, we made our own and then prepared to meet our lawyer. We had a piece of paper with his address and departed the condo with about thirty minutes to spare, although we had been told Claro's offices were nearby. We crossed the street and hailed a cab, indicating that we did not speak Spanish and handing him the piece of paper. The driver closely examined the address, looked at us, and then started speaking quickly, pointing down the road. Thinking he was asking us if he could proceed, we just kept nodding. He finally shrugged his shoulders, drove one block, turned left and stopped. We were at our destination, perhaps a two minute walk from the condo. The cab fare was about 50 cents. I gave him a big tip.

Our first meeting with Andres was most informative. He was a perfect choice for us – fluent in English and accustomed to dealing with North Americans investing in Chile. But he had not done a small real estate deal before. He was primarily a corporate lawyer dealing in large mining, infrastructure and other major business deals. However, he wanted to help and would do everything he could to protect our interests. We agreed to proceed, recognizing that his fees would be expensive, but also knowing that everything would be done correctly and properly.

Andres and Claro were instrumental and essential in helping us buy Castillo Verde. They provided sound, reasonable advice, were never confrontational (in my experience, the problem with many lawyers is their tendency to force adversarial positions to prolong a dispute and increase their fees), and always helpful.

Their claim to offer "full-service" legal advice was tested severely in our case, especially when Andres volunteered to accompany us to a large private clinic where Karen and I were to have a medical exam at our bank's request to support our mortgage with life insurance. As most of the people in the clinic did not speak English, Andres had offered to help ensure our visit went smoothly and that we did everything required. The challenge came when a nurse appeared with a small tin pan and a jar, handed them to Karen, pointed to the bathroom, and started talking rapidly in Spanish. Andres blushed a deep shade of red, but fortunately Karen, with practice gained in birthing three children, had provided enough urine samples in her past and did not need the instructions translated. Andres was visibly relieved.

One of the first lessons we learned from Andres was, when you buy and own a property in a foreign country, you must never say, or even think, "we sure don't do things this way back home". If you expect the rest of world to work the same way that it does at your original home, you will quickly go mad.

Take, for instance, the concept of property ownership in Chile. Back in Canada the process is fairly simple. You work with a real estate agent who helps you find and negotiate a purchase price for the home of your dreams. You then engage a real estate lawyer to prepare all the necessary papers and agreements and research titles to the property. As your agents, your real estate professional and your lawyer work on your behalf with the seller's counterparts to ensure the transaction moves smoothly, efficiently and rapidly to a close.

Taking this experience to Chile did not prove to be very successful. First, we did not have a real estate agent; they are few and far between in this country, and properties for sale seem to be marketed largely by word of mouth. Our law firm, one of the largest in Chile, apparently did not have anyone who specialized in real estate law. It seemed that to purchase a house in Chile, you agreed on a price, paid over the funds, and obtained the keys. If there was a problem with title or some other matter, well, one could clear them up later. When we made our deal with Carlos to purchase Castillo Verde, he certainly seemed to think this was what would happen. But he had underestimated these overly anal-retentive Canadians who wanted to make sure they really did own what they were purchasing.

In Chile there are three titles to real property ownership – *uso*, *goce* and *disposicion*. Roughly translated, the three rights are those of use, of enjoyment, and the ability to sell a property. The challenge is that all three rights are separate and can be held by different people. In one example a friend of ours selling a condominium in Santiago realized at the last minute that the person who had originally sold him the property three years before had not included the *disposicion*, the right to sell, in the original transaction. In order to complete the current sale of his property, our friend had to race across the city on the day of the closing to have the right to sell transferred by the original owner, who was in hospital dying of cancer. Fortunately, he arrived in time, the original owner was able to assign the right of sale to our friend, and the deal went ahead.

They sure don't do things that way in Canada!

Normally the first two rights, those to be able to use and enjoy a property, come together in what is called *usofructo*. The derivation of the word comes from the Latin *usus*, the right of use, and *fructus*, or the fruits of the property. The concept of *usofructo* was first enshrined in Roman law where it was a type of servitude that provided the legal right to use and derive profit or benefit from a property that belonged to another person. The *usofrucuary* did not have real possession of the property, but had the right to use and enjoy it as well as the right to receive profits from any replenishable commodity situated on it. A *usofrucuary* could even sell his *usofructo*, but not the actual ownership of the property.

Now that you are clear on all of this, imagine our concern when we learned that, well into the process of purchasing Castillo Verde, the three rights of ownership of the property actually resided with two people in the seller's family. Taking this to a logical extreme, if we had purchased Castillo Verde in the transaction that Carlos had expected, it would have been possible for his brother to turn up with his children and a tent enforcing his right to use the property, while another family member could arrive to harvest the Castillo's various fruit trees to take home.

Apparently, most properties are owned in this manner in Chile, and while we seemed to be able to obtain the first two rights – to use and enjoy - the right to sell (*disposicion*) was becoming increasingly difficult to get. We believe this right was held by Carlos' mother, and we all know how challenging relationships between moms and their sons can be.

Fortunately, after many months of discussions between Andres and Carlos' lawyer, all of the various rights were accumulated and we were ready to formalize the purchase of Castillo Verde. Unfortunately, we then learned, there were a few more hurdles to cross, issues that would take another eight months to correct.

CHAPTER FIVE

BLOOD HAS BEEN SPILLED OVER WATER

I n addition to obtaining all of the rights of ownership to Castillo Verde, another reason for the long delay in actually receiving the deed was the question of water rights.

During the transition period as ownership was being transferred to us, Carlos discovered new regulations were being enforced by the local municipality that would not allow property transfers to occur without inspections being done and approvals given for water, sewage, gas and electrical systems. The inspections performed on Castillo Verde revealed a number of shortcomings and issues that need to be rectified. These projects took quite a few months as Carlos appeared to use the cheapest materials and labour – probably the son of his best-friend's uncle or some such person – to make the necessary modifications.

The largest issue was the water system.

Chile possesses one of the best coverage and quality levels for their water and sanitation systems in all of Latin America. Beginning in the early 1970's, and extending well into the 1990's, the country embarked on a massive infrastructure renewal project focused on water systems. As state-owned utilities improved their efficiency and became self-financing, under the Pinochet regime they were gradually turned over to the private sector. Today, almost all urban water systems in Chile are privately owned and operated, and all are overseen by government authorities with strict regulations and subsidy programs for the poor. The World Health Organization has recognized Chile's water privatization as exemplary, and considers it a model for other countries to follow, including those in Europe.

This modern and efficient system, however, has only been applied in the major urban centres of the country. The vast rural areas of Chile have not been included in these modernization and privatization processes, where local water cooperatives and water boards supply services. In many of these areas, Chileans lack adequate potable water connections. Castillo Verde was just such a location.

The town in which Castillo Verde is situated is nominally serviced by *Aguas de Pirque*, a local water board that obtains and treats the water for its residents from mountain streams. Unfortunately, the extent of their service area ended at the wrong side of a bridge just below our property. We investigated extending a connection from Castillo Verde to the termination of their service, but the cost was prohibitive, and subsequently we learned that the quality of the water from *Aguas de Pirque* was suspect. We decided to depend on the current water system, an unincorporated and loosely formed water cooperative, a *Comunidad de Aguas* of approximately fourteen member properties surrounding Parque McKenna. Officially known as the *Comunidad de Aguas Fundo Parque de San Juan de Pirque*, it had been designed and organized by the original owners of the Parque. Castillo Verde owned one share in the *Comunidad*.

Parque Mackenna was carved out of the Andean wilderness in the mid-1800's to house one of Chile's more prominent families during the summer months. The main house, a large and typical Chilean hacienda, included approximately twenty rooms on one extensive floorplan surrounded by a wide, covered terrace. Typically, all of the rooms were connected to each other on the inside, and each had a door to the outside terrace. The house was surrounded by huge Chilean palms, and situated in front were two large ponds with impressive fountains and water features. A consecrated chapel was positioned to the east of the main house, and a number of other buildings were constructed on the property to house the staff and guests. One of the more grand guest house constructions was our own Castillo Verde.

During the time we were purchasing Castillo Verde, the main house in Parque Mackenna was also available. As is typical in Chile, there were no real details about the property easily available to prospective purchasers, although we did learn that the price for the property ran from US $1 million to $3 million – we kept hearing different prices depending on who we asked. The property was being looked after by John Cassen, a descendant of the Mackenna family, on behalf of his siblings who owned the house and grounds.

Like many Chileans, John used his dogs as the main security force for the Parque, and a number of these large brutes could be seen prowling the grounds day and night. Untypically, among the pack of dogs was a large fluffy white sheep. Apparently John had adopted this sheep as a small lamb and, growing up with his dogs without the company of other sheep, it had acquired more dog-like characteristics than its sheep-like genealogy. One of these traits was its propensity to jealously guard the property.

On one of our visits Marcela offered to take us on a tour of the Parque, and contacted John who met us at the gate to open the property. As we were walking up the driveway, a number of the dogs came to see what was up but, as John was with us, they moved away. Except for the sheep who, mistaking us for intruders, ran at Karen and knocked her down. It then attacked Marcela who was also injured in the fracas. John quickly corralled the sheep, and as an apology, offered to make us a lamb stew from the animal's remains. We declined, but Karen still has a dent in the side of her thigh from the head butt.

Victoria Mackenna, although merely the wife of the owner, actually ruled the home and the property with a strong hand, and as the property was gradually divided during the turn of the century, all of the various properties needed potable water. This necessary life-force came from a series of pipes fed from mountain springs high up in the Andes into a reservoir which, in turn, funneled the water into a long canal that wound part way down the mountains to a large tank. From this tank a large pipe led to the Parque, from which Mrs. Mackenna decided who should get water, and how much.

She was actually quite fair in her treatment and allocation of this precious resource, but she always had the option of simply turning the tap off. It was the ultimate power in the neighbourhood, and apparently she used it to make sure she got her way. There are stories about quite violent disputes, and we have been told that "blood has been spilled over fights for this water."

Into this fray we gullible Canadians walked, expecting that water was always available, just like at home. Canada possesses one of the most abundant fresh water resources in the world, and we have become accustomed to treating water as a right more than a privilege. But this was not the case in Chile, and three years later we were still trying to obtain some sort of formal agreement that says we have purchased the right to this water supply. Apparently no such formal agreement exists for anyone, although there is a gathering force of local residents attempting to formalize our loose alliance of water users from the Parque into a registered body with exclusive access to our water system.

At Castillo Verde there are two sources of water we needed to worry about. One is derived directly from the Maipo River through a series of canals extending along the roadways and across hillsides throughout our neighbourhood. This water supply is used exclusively for irrigating the gardens. It is a dark brown, silt-filled flow that arrives at the Castillo from the Maipo River via uncovered channels and into a large cistern at the back of our property. From there it is pumped through various hoses and pipes extending around the property to irrigate the gardens. The second source, the potable water used for the house, arrives by a small plastic hose from the center of Parque McKenna.

When the municipality first inspected the potable water system at Castillo Verde, they were surprised to discover that the water was untreated. It is the responsibility of each property owner within these rural cooperatives to ensure their water is properly chlorinated and filtered for safe consumption. These municipal inspections were a relatively new innovation and were aimed at bringing some control and regulation into these loose associations. Carlos was forced to improve the water supply before he would be allowed to transfer ownership to us.

The original system saw the water arrive from the Parque into a large cistern and then pumped into an ancient tank sitting on a rotting wooden platform about ten feet above the ground. The height and position of the tank was designed to provide adequate gravity-induced pressure to service the Castillo. Both the cistern and the tank were supposed to be covered and secure to ensure nothing fell in to contaminate the water. Unfortunately, both were open to the elements, with cracked and unused covers placed off to the side as well as screening so clotted with dead leaves and branches as to be virtually useless. There were no filters or treatment systems anywhere to be seen.

As a solution, Carlos installed an old pump he had scavenged from the swimming pool and inserted it into the system between the cistern and a new, much smaller treatment tank, bypassing the high tank that previously had provided the water pressure. In theory, when water was requested by the house, the new pump would turn on, bring water from the cistern into the new tank where chlorine was added, and then into the house. The problem was the system's capacity – a request for one shower, or the flushing of a couple of toilets, would quickly drain the small treatment tank and, as a result, water to the house would be shut off until a full tank had been treated, Somehow, Carlos received approval for this system – we believe he must have known someone to get this done. As soon as we finally owned Castillo Verde, we hired a contractor to install an entirely new system with much larger tanks, pumps, treatment facilities and a larger diameter service pipe to the house.

And while this new and improved system functions very well, unless you want to lose a lot of weight and fluids, I would not recommend drinking our water unless it is first boiled. While safe, the water is so rich in minerals and other ingredients that, North Americans unaccustomed to this richness, often find their digestive systems somewhat taxed. Such is life in rural Chile.

CHAPTER SIX
CHILE CAN BE A BIT BUREAUCRATIC

mong our first tasks after agreeing to purchase Castillo Verde was to acquire the use of our own vehicle. Pancho and Angela had kindly offered us the use of one of their trucks, but it quickly became apparent that with the frequency of our visits, and the number of times we had to meet with our lawyers and bankers or shop in local stores, we would soon outlive our welcome.

Contrary to what you might believe, driving in Chile is quite civilized. Unlike the horrors of attempting to navigate through Mexico, Brazil or Argentina, drivers in Chile are very law abiding. For the most part they obey speed limits, and, unlike most North American drivers, generally understand the importance of lane markers, turn signals, brakes, and all the other modern technologies included in today's motor vehicle.

However, while driving may be quite painless for the average North American, obtaining the means to travel the country's highways and by-ways was not.

On another of our visits we arrived mid-morning on Boxing Day, the day after Christmas. I had assumed it would be easy to rent a car at the airport, a normal and simple task in most cities. Despite finding a row of familiar car rental agencies in booths manned by the standard, fresh-faced and smiling young people, none had any vehicles available. There was not one car, truck or van of any size or description for rent at what is one of South America's largest airports. Hertz, Avis, Budget, Dollar and all the other brands should take note – nothing was available at any price. As we walked away from the friendly but unhelpful booths, we were accosted by a number of men who claimed to act for car rental agencies located in the city. They had pictures and rate cards for vehicles apparently available and offered to take us to their offices. We had been warned to avoid these unauthorized bandits, and declined. We hailed a taxi to take us to our friends' house in Pirque and asked them to employ their skills to obtain a vehicle for us.

For most of us, renting a car is fairly easy. You contact one of the major rental companies by phone or over the Internet, confirm a booking at an airport or downtown location, give them credit card and driver's license numbers, and all you need do is show up, provide some identification, fill in some paperwork, and you are shuttled off to a clean, fully-fueled vehicle in first-class condition. The process from start to finish might take fifteen minutes.

Not so in Chile, as I discovered. I have tried not to bring more meaning to my experience of renting a car in Santiago, however the adventure is worth relating as it does help to set the stage, both for the state of mind necessary to proceed with our adventure, but also to explain how one must develop a sense of humour when living in a foreign country.

It was the Friday of the New Year's weekend, and we needed a car to attend a party in Colchagua about two hours south of Santiago. Sergio had booked a vehicle for us at Dollar Car Rental and provided my driver's license, passport number and credit card information over the phone – everything you would expect an agency to want to ensure a smooth and effortless transaction. The office was kind enough to provide us with the name of the only agent at the location fluent in English.

As I entered the agency office, I was greeted by a scene of mass chaos and confusion. People were lined up six and ten deep, all gesticulating, muttering loudly and waving papers. Four harried agents behind a counter were filling in paperwork, answering phones, and looking outside the windows for help. None came.

This was also my introduction to queuing in South America. In short, you don't. You stand in the crowd, elbow and push your way forward, trying not to be the victim as everyone else attempts to get in front of you.

As I worked my way into the middle of the crowd after about thirty minutes, I vainly tried to determine which clerk was Alfredo – the agent with the gift of the English language. It was impossible to tell as everyone in the line was speaking Spanish. When I finally attained the desk, I was astonished to discover that the agent I had reached was actually the English-speaking Alfredo. The bad news was that he had not heard of me, there was no paperwork for me, and no car was ready. We had to start all over again.

The rental agreement, insurance information and other demands went well, and after a lengthy wait outside, my mid-sized car was delivered. During the walk-through, I was told the cover for the seatbelt latch was missing, but not to worry, everything worked. I jumped in and drove away. What they did not tell me was that, with this cover missing, the seatbelt warning system would not recognize that the latch was fastened, and would emit its loud and obnoxious beeping for at least fifteen minutes every time the car was started, and for three consecutive times while driving. They also did not tell me that the air conditioning, and indeed the entire ventilation system for the vehicle, did not function.

After three days of headache inducing seatbelt warning chimes, and driving on some very dusty roads in plus 30 degree Celsius temperatures with no air conditioning and the windows rolled up, I determined I had to return to the agency to exchange the car. Back I went.

You can imagine my dismay when the same mob scene greeted me at the agency. It appeared that returning a rental car in Chile demands much more than dropping the keys and mileage into a box – the car must be examined before your charges are calculated. Into the fray I went, my frustration mounting.

Fortunately the same English-speaking agent was at the desk to meet me and tried to be helpful. He listened to my story, and pointed to a man just walking out the door, explaining that I must show him the problem and properly return the car before it could be replaced. I hastened outside through the mass of people, only to find the man had disappeared. I am sure he was hiding from me; as I soon learned, I was not alone in wanting to replace my rental vehicle.

I walked all over the lot and offices, but he was no where to be found. Back I went into the office, only to find I needed to again wait through the lineup to reach my agent. After another thirty minutes, he was most apologetic, and found someone to come with me. I clung to him and out we went. The car was inspected, the deficiencies noted, and an agreement was made that another vehicle would be provided. I was told to go back in and the agent would fill out the paperwork for the new car.

Again, I had to fight my way through the never-diminishing gang of people to reach Alfredo. However, this time I decided to go with the flow and talk to my fellow renters to understand why they were joining me in the line. One group was trying to get their third replacement vehicle. Their most recent van had encountered a brake failure. I had seen this vehicle during my frequent trips around the rental yard - two men had been pounding heavily at the rear brake shoe with a sledge hammer. The client, seeing this high quality repair work, had asked for another vehicle. A second fellow renter told me they had picked up their vehicle, only to have it run out of gas five seconds from the agency. They were waiting for the firm to push it back into the lot, and then to go and obtain gasoline. They had been waiting two hours.

All in all, it took me four hours to obtain my replacement vehicle, this time with functioning seat belts, climate and ventilation systems. The interior lights did not illuminate, but I did not care by this point.

As I drove back to Pirque, I thought I would investigate the cost of a used vehicle. There was what looked like a reputable dealer lot not far from the rental agency, and I pulled in to investigate. A very pleasant salesman discussed the prices of a few vehicles at hand with me, most of which seemed reasonable. I had been warned that one must be very careful when purchasing a used vehicle in Chile. Apparently, mining companies were notorious for taking their abused, bent, damaged and un-maintained trucks, re-painting them, and then asking for top dollar in the Santiago used-vehicle market. The salesman then surprised me by saying that if I wanted to rent any of his vehicles for a week or so, it would be simple. Apparently this was a normal event when considering the purchase of a used vehicle. I almost strangled him.

To ensure we would not encounter this rental nightmare again, we decided to acquire our own vehicle as soon as possible. Fortunately, one of the fine people we had met at the Canadian embassy in Santiago was being posted to another country and wanted to sell his Toyota RAV

4 to a willing purchaser. The vehicle had been brought from Canada and driven only by this person – it had been well maintained, had low mileage and, best of all, it was green in colour, a positive omen as it would be residing at Castillo Verde. We agreed on a price and the truck was ours, or so I thought.

Because the vehicle had been imported from Canada by a diplomat and had been driven with diplomatic plates, the vehicle did not really exist in the Chilean license registration system. Our lawyer expended a number of very expensive hours contacting the various authorities to ensure the transfer could proceed, and on our next trip I was presented with the necessary papers and license plates to get everything done.

The first stop was a visit to the Revisión Técnica, government-run garages located throughout the country at which every vehicle must be inspected annually for mechanical fitness and emissions control. This is a great idea and should be done everywhere in the world as the inspections ensure unsafe or polluting vehicles are taken off the road until they are repaired. Unfortunately in Chile it was clearly evident that the system did not apply to buses and most other commercial vehicles. Smog was an endemic problem in Santiago.

The issue with Chile's inspection system is that the licenses, and thus the dates for inspection for all vehicles, occur only two times per year. As a result, approximately half of all Chilean vehicles arrive at these inspection stations on one of these two dates, and apparently I had arrived on one such very busy day.

We waited about an hour in a long line until we reached an official who informed us that they could not inspect the vehicle because the license plates were not attached. I pulled the plates out and showed him that we had them with us, and perhaps one of their mechanics could fix them to car for us during its inspection. Unfortunately, this task was not in their job description, and we had to leave our place in line, exit the facility, find a mechanic, have the plates attached to the bumpers, and then re-join the line again.

After passing the mechanical fitness examination at the Revisión Técnica, we had to obtain a local license. I don't really understand what this is, but apparently, in addition to the license plates attached to the vehicle and the national registration this represents, you also have to register your vehicle in a community – it does not matter which, although most people apply where they live. Fortunately, we selected a community office where there were no lines, although we arrived at 2.00 pm just as the office closed for lunch - for two hours. We shrugged and went off for lunch ourselves. Returning at 4.00, we provided the appropriate papers and after much scrutiny, discussion, photocopying, computer data entry, filling out of forms and telephone conversations, we were told the license was fine, but we needed to pay for it at another kiosk outside and down the hall, and then return with proof of payment to acquire the certificate.

Chileans are great at this – you select something you want to buy or acquire, you then pay at another location, and return to retrieve your purchases. It employs a lot of people, which I guess is the point.

The final step was to acquire a transponder for the highway systems. Most of the major highways in Chile are toll roads, and in and around Santiago every vehicle is required to have a transponder to ensure appropriate charges are collected. With all our papers in hand, we traveled out to one of the kiosks set up to deliver and register these transponders. After standing in another extensive and hot lineup, we were told they could not give me one as I did not have a residency permit or anything that told them where they could mail an invoice. I tried to have them use my lawyer's address, but this was not acceptable as I had no identification with this address. Finally, our lawyers' mother, Haydee, who had become an indispensable part of our Chilean support team, returned with our SUV on her own and had the transponder registered at her address.

Thus, after almost three days, we could legally drive our car.

The bureaucratic tendency of Chileans was reinforced when we purchased the appliances for Castillo Verde. We had done a bit of research and determined we would obtain the best selection of products and, we surmised, the best levels of service, at one of the country's major department stores. In the company of the patient Haydee, we made our way to one of the larger branches of the *Paris Almacen* empire, among the largest network of retailers in Chile. We had visited the store the day prior and decided to purchase all of our appliances – refrigerator, stove, dishwasher, clothes washer and dryer – from the same manufacturer and the same retailer so that we would have a uniform look in our kitchen as well as one source for installation and service.

The first hurdle occurred when the man helping us realized that we wanted to pay for everything with one payment on our Canadian-issued American Express credit card. In Chile, almost everyone purchases large-ticket items in *cuotas*, a series of monthly payments with exorbitant interest rates attached. We were highly unusual in that we did not want to avail ourselves of this privilege. Apparently, for one of the country's largest retail chains, they had never experienced someone wanting to pay for so many items at such a high total price at one time with one payment on one credit card. As a result, there were an endless series of phone calls with increasingly senior levels of store management, all of whom, although not appearing to distrust us, were mystified about our purchase and the method of payment. Finally, we reached a person with sufficient authority to authorize the transaction, and the charge was put through to American Express.

American Express, of course, refused to honour the charge without telephone verification, and the second hurdle to our purchase was initiated. We had not used this credit card in Chile up to now, and American Express were concerned our request was a case of identity theft and they simply would not accept the transaction. We called them, but we could not reach anyone in their management structure who could authorize the purchase. Apparently there was a department somewhere who handled these issues, but nothing we did would get us through to them. After several frustrating calls and conversations, we decided to use our Visa card to make the purchase. Oddly enough, two days later American Express called us to inquire about the purchase, wondering if there was a problem they could help resolve. We returned their credit card to them.

The decision to change credit cards, of course, resulted in further consternation and concern with the Paris Almacen management team. Why had our purchase been refused? Was there a problem? Who were these Canadians, really? We had to start all over again, talking to the store's management, explaining why we were changing credit cards, and convincing them it was not our problem, but that of American Express.

I became so frustrated I retired to the store's mattress department down the hall for a nap.

Finally, with Haydee's controlled anger and Karen near to tears with rage at both the store and the credit card companies, the purchase was authorized by Visa and we had a delivery date for our appliances. The entire payment process had taken more than six hours.

CHAPTER SEVEN

DIEZ Y OCHO, SEPTIEMBRE

n addition to a lot of dogs, Chile also has a lot of holidays. They say that Chile has more public holidays during the year than any other South American country, and I am sure they are correct given the number of times we telephoned to our builder and architect, or visited the job site during the restoration of Castillo Verde, only to find no one around as it was either before, after or during another national holiday.

Adding to the standard holidays of Christmas, Good Friday, Easter, and New Year's Day, Chileans celebrate Labour Day in early May and Navy Day later in the same month, a day off for Saint Peter and Saint Paul in June, one for Our Lady of Mount Carmel in July, the Assumption of Mary in August, an Army Day in September, Columbus Day in October, All Saints Day in November and the Immaculate Conception in early December. In total, there are fourteen statutory days off work in the Chilean calendar, not including the practice of taking additional days off prior to and after some of the more important dates. I remember as a child asking if my family could convert to Judaism as they not only got to disappear from school for their own special religious holidays while we remained rooted in our lessons, they also were able to celebrate the statutory Christian holidays the rest of us enjoyed. In retrospect, I should have asked to move to Chile. With this wealth of monthly holidays dotted throughout the year, our days away from the classroom would have been much more frequent.

The granddaddy of all Chilean holidays is *Fiestas Patrias*, celebrated on the eighteenth of September each year. The festival includes two official public holidays – September 18, commemorating the proclamation of the first governing junta in the country in 1810 that began the process of gaining full independence from the Spanish, and September 19, known as the *Dia de las Glorias del Ejército*, or the Day of the Glories of the Chilean Army.

Depending on what weekday the eighteenth of September lands on, the holidays can last a full week, and children can find themselves away from the rigours of school for up to two full weeks. Next to Christmas, *Fiestas Patrias* is the most important holiday in the Chilean calendar, and all businesses close, as well as banks, government offices and shops - almost everyone takes time off to celebrate. The key exceptions are restaurants, bars and clubs as wine, beer, pisco, food, music and dancing are integral components of this annual celebration.

Since 1967 it is also a law that every public building must fly a Chilean flag during the *Fiestas Patrias*, punishable with fines of up to 40,000 pesos, or about Canadian $80, if the rules are not followed. While I am not sure if this legislation extends to residences and businesses, it seems like everyone participates by demonstrating their patriotism and displaying the Chilean flag somewhere on their property. To meet demand for the banner, and because the law states that each flag flown must be pristine, everywhere you turn during the weeks leading up to the big day you will find people selling the Chilean flag in all sorts of forms – large ones for flying from your house, small ones for your car, tee-shirts to wear, stickers to place on your belongings, kites to fly, anything that can be decorated with the colorful flag is available on roadsides and in shops. As you drive around the cities and countryside, it is quite something to see row on row of the red, white and blue flag with the white star in the upper left hand corner waving proudly in the breeze.

Chilean independence was officially declared on February 12, 1818, however the process took a number of years to complete, beginning on September 18, 1810, the day that is now celebrated throughout the country.

In 1808 Spain had been invaded by France under its Emperor Napoleon, and the country that had held Chile under an iron fist for centuries was in a state of turmoil. The Chilean people, who had already been agitating for some form of home rule, were very aware of the state of affairs in Europe. Magnifying the opportunity was the authoritarian and disdainful manner in which the new Governor of Chile, Francisco Garcia Carrasco, ruled the country. Both the landowning elite in Chile, and the armed forces that kept the Spanish in power, had had enough, and they came together to propose that the Spanish government be replaced by a "junta of noble citizens of Chile". An open meeting to discuss the proposal was set for September 18, 1810.

The move toward full Chilean independence began at this meeting, and historians have divided the process into three stages - *Patria Vieja, Reconquista,* and *Patria Nueva* - all of which involved a series of battles between the pro-independence forces and the Spanish Royalists

At the September 18 meeting, the Spanish acceded to the demands of the *juntistas* and, in handing them the ceremonial baton of rule, initiated what is now known as the *Patria Vieja* period. To move the process forward, it was decided at the open meeting to hold elections for a National Congress in early 1811. As the election day approached, a Royalist by the name of Tomás de Figueroa led a revolt in Santiago that was summarily defeated and its leader executed. However, the revolt temporarily sabotaged the elections, delaying them until November, with the Moderates, who advocated only a modicum of greater autonomy from Spain, but not full independence, winning a majority of seats.

Political intrigue was rampant throughout the country following these elections, culminating in two coups at the end of 1811 that resulted in a more pro-independence government under José Miguel Carrera and Bernardo O'Higgins. Remember that last name; it is very important in Chilean history and you will find streets named after him in almost every Chilean city and town.

The move toward total independence gained further momentum during this period. A law was passed that "no order that emanates from outside Chile will have any effect, and anyone who enforces such an order will be declared a traitor". A new flag for the country was introduced, Chile's first pro-independence newspaper began publishing, and links to the new liberalism and federalism of the United States were forged with the establishment of the first US consul to Chile.

These developments in Chile, as well as additional moves toward independence in neighbouring Argentina, were viewed with concern by the Spanish Viceroy of Peru, who sent a military force by sea to deal with the upstart Chileans and protect Spanish interests. Landing unopposed at Concepción, they marched south toward Santiago but were partially repulsed by the Chileans under Carrera and O'Higgins in what turned out to be a not very decisive victory. In particular, Carrera's shortcomings as a military leader were very evident.

With its unconvincing defeat, the Spanish decided to sign the Treaty of Lircay on May 14, 1813. However they had no intention of honouring the peace treaty and immediately sent a much larger Royalist force under the direction of Spanish General Mariano Osorio to quell the Chilean uprising. They moved into Chillán to the south of Santiago and demanded full surrender. O'Higgins wanted to defend the city of Rancagua, between Chillán and Santiago, but Carrera pushed for a defence closer to the city at Angostura. As a result, the independence forces were badly divided, and O'Higgins was soundly defeated in the Disaster at Rancagua over the first two days of October, 1814. Of his 5,000 troops that entered the battle, only 500 survived, including O'Higgins. The Spanish forces then moved north and entered Santiago unopposed, ending the *Patria Vieja* period of Chilean independence.

The second period, *Reconquista*, began with the confirmation of the Spanish General Mariano Osorio as governor of Chile. He and his successors embarked on a campaign of fierce political repression to teach the upstart Chileans a lesson, sending hundreds into exile and killing many, including a number of members of the 1810 junta. O'Higgins and Carrera escaped to Mendoza, a province of the newly independent Argentina, just to the east of Santiago on the other side of the formidable Andes Mountains.

While in exile, the Chilean patriots joined forces with José de San Martin, the leader of the Argentinean independence movement and now Governor of Mendoza. San Martin favoured the military expertise of O'Higgins over the inept track record of Carrera, and over the next three years they organized an army to re-cross the Andes and recapture Santiago. On February 12, 1817 they defeated the Royalist forces in the Battle of Chacabuco to the north of Santiago and triumphantly reentered the city. To ensure a smooth transition and to prevent any conflict, San Martin turned down the position of Supreme Director of Chile and appointed O'Higgins as its first leader, a post he retained until

1823. On the first anniversary of the Battle of Chacabuco, O'Higgins formally declared independence from Spain, launching the third and final phase, *Patria Nueva*.

The Spanish were nothing if not dogged in their pursuit of Chile, and in 1818 another Royalist force under Mariano Osorio was sent to Concepcion north of Santiago with orders to march south and retake the city. They soundly defeated the Chileans at the Battle of Cancha Rayda on March 18, 1818, following which O'Higgins delegated command of his troops to the Argentinean leader José de San Martin. Just under a month later, on April 5, San Martin inflicted a decisive victory over the Spanish forces at the Battle of Maipú, on the outskirts of Santiago, and the Spanish retreated, never again to launch a major offensive against Chile.

In the following years San Martin, at the request of O'Higgins, launched a series of battles against armed bandits, royalists, and native Indians who had used the period of instability to further their own gains. As he worked to establish internal stability, O'Higgins took a number of steps to ensure Chile could defend itself from any further foreign invasion. As a first step, he founded the Chilean navy, placing the famous Scottish Admiral Lord Thomas Cochrane in charge. You should also remember that name as he too has streets named after him in almost every Chilean town and city. In 1820 Cochrane won a decisive victory over the remaining Royalist forces in a successful attack of the fortifications at Valdivia, following which he landed a force in northern Chiloé to defeat the last Spanish stronghold in the country.

With these victories, a shaky independence was finally achieved, strengthened when Peru was finally liberated from the Spanish by Simon Bolivar in late 1824. The *Patria Nueva* period of Chilean self-rule is considered to have ended with the resignation of O'Higgins in 1823 and the institution of formal elections.

The celebration of the *Festias Patrias* on September 18 embraces the entire country of Chile, and includes parades, festivals, food, music and much drinking. Many of these events are held in *ramadas*, or large open air buildings constructed specifically for the celebrations, and include a dance floor under a thatched roof or one traditionally made of tree branches. *Asados*, or open pit barbecues, are everywhere, and the scent of baked *empanadas* fills the air. Chilean rodeos are held in the town's *medialuna*, a semi-circular arena, where local *huasos* display their horsemanship by guiding a steer through a series of defined movements. Traditional folklore and crafts are on display, kites are flown, games are played, cooking demonstrations held, families with their children enjoy the celebrations, and everyone dances the *cueca*.

The *cueca* was declared the national dance of Chile on September 18, 1979, and can be found everywhere people gather. The dance attempts to re-enact the courting ritual of a rooster and a hen, asking the male dancer to be aggressive in attitude while the woman is elusive, demure and defensive. The dance steps are formulaic, but can vary from region to region. Many dancers use a scarf or handkerchief as an element of their performance to be waived and employed as a disguise. The dancing is beautiful to watch, and the music, played on guitars and brass instruments, often accompanied by voices telling a story, is infectious. One cannot avoid the tapping of toes, and even standing and moving to the hypnotic rhythms.

Our first encounter with *la cueca* occurred at a party Pancho held at his house and studio during a rainy winter night in August. It was a celebration of a friend's birthday, and a number of Pancho's students who attended were also professional *cueca* musicians. As I had stupidly told Pancho I was taking drum lessons in Canada, he had exaggerated my level of skill to his friends and I was invited to join their *cueca* band as its percussionist. I suppose they had expected me to bring my own drum kit, and when I turned up with nothing, improvisation took over and I was given a cheese grater and steel knife to grind out the complicated *cueca* rhythms. After some instruction, and listening to a few of their songs, I slowly got the hang of things and managed a couple of decent sets before retiring my rudimentary instruments to one of the more practiced members of the group. It was my first gig as a musician - I use the term very loosely - but I will treasure the evening in my memory for years to come.

Coincidently, September is also the month in which Chileans elected Salvador Allende as the world's first Marxist head of state in 1970, and it is also the month in which Augusto Pinochet staged his military coup to overthrow Allende's government. As a result, you may find that the

Patria Nueva holiday may include demonstrations by supporters on both sides of this delicate issue, and care needs to be taken not to get caught in protests. However, these demonstrations are becoming few and far between as time heals the Chilean people's wounds, and happy celebrations are mostly prevalent.

On our first *Patria Nueva* visit to Chile, we took the opportunity to visit Valparaiso, Chile's main port city situated about two hours west of Santiago. The drive to Valparaiso is worth the time in itself as, once leaving the sprawl and smog of Santiago, you move through the fertile plains of the Casablanca wine valley, noted for its Cabernet Sauvignon and Chardonnay grapes and home to many of Chile's finest wineries. As you climb up a coastal cordillera, you enter a long tunnel to emerge into a wooded hilly region that descends slowly toward the coast. The hills are covered with native coniferous trees, including the famed araucaria tree, or "monkey puzzle", found only in Chile. Dotted throughout these pine forests are numerous majestic Chilean palms towering over their neighbours. It is a beautiful and peaceful drive. And because it was the *Patria Nueva* holiday, at the summit of one very tall palm flew the Chilean flag. It must have been a very precarious climb to place it there.

Valparaiso itself is situated on a series of some 45 steep hills forming a natural amphitheatre overlooking a beautiful harbour on the Pacific coast. Founded in 1536 by Juan de Saavedra while searching for a location to land troops, the city was officially named Valparaiso in 1544 by Pedro de Valdivia. As a port city, and for generations a port of call for ships from around the world, Valparaiso contains one of the most ethnically mixed populations in the country, including people from France, England, Scotland, Portugal, Italy, Germany, Yugoslavia and many other countries. In 2003 the city was designated as a UNESCO World Heritage Site.

Ironically, two of the people most entwined in Chile's recent past were born in Valparaiso. Both Salvador Allende and Augusto Pinochet were raised in this colourful port city and attended the same junior school. I wonder whose picture adorns the wall of this institution celebrating its illustrious alumni.

It is difficult to describe the steepness of the streets in this city without first hand experience. Many cannot be managed by any vehicle, and Chileans claim that the women of Valparaiso have the best-looking legs in the country as they must walk up and down these steep hillsides on a daily basis. As we struggled, panting and sweating, up and down some of these streets, I wondered how on earth municipal services such as water, electricity and sewage handling could function efficiently on these grades, especially given the prevalence of earthquakes in the area. And if there were a fire or other emergency, I would hope to live on or near a passage more navigable by a vehicle.

Houses are perched everywhere, one on top of another, with no consistent architecture, and all are painted different hues forming a rainbow of colour as one looks out from the numerous *miradores*, or lookouts perched atop the hills. In addition to the more roughly-built houses, there are also many stately mansions constructed by the wealthy traders, bankers and politicians who founded the city and have since called it their home. Most are neo-classic and European in design, befitting the English and German businessmen who helped to build the city's economy.

As an alternative to walking, there are at least nine elevators, or funiculars, dotted around the city that can be used to ascend to the top of centrally-situated hills. The oldest, the Barón Elevator, was built in 1906 and was the world's first to use an electric motor rather than the gravitational effect of the downward car to move passengers to the top. It is a dangerous looking affair, antique right down to the ticket booth and entrance, but the ride is quite safe with spectacular views of the harbour, the ocean and the surrounding hills of the city.

Valparaiso is known for its seafood. Small restaurants dot the shore and up the hills surrounding the harbour, where one can enjoy the freshest catch of the day along with Chile's finest wines and spectacular views. Our favorite is the *Bote Salvavidas* situated directly on the harbour. It is named after the lifeboat society that is on constant alert in the event of an emergency on sea, and the society's flags and pictures of it in action are displayed throughout the restaurant.

As in most Chilean seafood establishments, at the *Bote Salvavidas* a diner makes three choices when ordering fish. The first decision is which fish to order from an extensive list, followed by how you want it cooked - grilled, baked, or fried - and finally what kind of sauce you want it served with. You can then order side dishes of potatos, rice and vegetables, although take care as the servings can be quite large. And when paying, remember that you must tell the waiter how much gratuity to add to your bill before they take your credit card away. The customary tip is between 10% and 15% of your total bill.

At the top of the Barón Elevator sits Chile's Naval Museum, built in 1842 overlooking the country's main naval base and barracks. The museum offers a number of fascinating exhibits, including a collection of torpedoes displayed in its central courtyard. I have not seen a real torpedo before, and they are terrifying. I can't imagine what it would be like to be sitting in the middle of the cold ocean watching one of these explosive-laden behemoths powering toward my ship.

One of the more interesting displays in the museum focuses on the Battle of Iquique, one of the central naval engagements with the Peruvian fleet during the War of the Pacific. When war was declared, the Chileans quickly moved a number of ships in their armada, including the wood-constructed corvette Esmeralda, to blockade the port of Iquique in the far north and stop any movement of Peruvian or Bolivian soldiers south toward Chile. To remove the blockade, the Peruvians sent their best fighting ships, among them the iron clad Huascar, to meet the Chileans. At 8.00 am on May 21, 1879 the Peruvian fleet arrived at Iquique and demanded the surrender of the clearly outmanned and outgunned Chileans. The Chileans refused, and both navies prepared for battle.

The main skirmish was fought between Chile's Esmeralda, under Captain Arturo Prat (of course, there are numerous streets nearing Prat's name throughout Chile), and Peru's Huascar, led by the Peruvian Commander Grau. Standing close to each other, both ships fired on the other with their main guns as well as with rifles and pistols manned by sailors sitting in the masts and riggings. Finally, about 10.30 am, one of the Huascar's shells penetrated the wooden hull of the Esmeralda killing all of the engineering crew and rendering the ship immobile. In return, the Esmeralda's missiles were unable to effectively pierce the iron sides of its opponent. Grau then decided to finish off the Chilean corvette by ramming the Esmeralda, one of their key naval tactics. It took three runs to sink the Chilean ship, but by 12.10 in the afternoon the Esmeralda broke in half and disappeared below the waves.

During one of the final collisions, Arturo Prat entered the lexicon of Chilean heroes by jumping aboard the Peruvian ship, along with one of his officers, and moving sword in hand toward the ship's bridge. He was immediately shot dead, as was his officer who died trying to throw a burning lamp at a wooden deck to start a fire. In total, the Chileans lost 135 sailors during the battle, although Grau saved 62 Chilean survivors from drowning.

As with many Chilean heroes, they don't seem to gain any recognition unless they suffer a major defeat, and Prat is no exception. Despite losing the battle and his ship, there is an entire room in the Naval Museum devoted to his life, with pictures of his childhood and family, his years at the Naval Academy, artifacts from his various postings, and many other elements. There are also two large scale models of each of the ships – the Esmeralda and the Huascar, with the latter being donated by the Peruvian Navy. As with Cochrane and O'Higgins, streets throughout the country are named after Arturo Prat.

Directly to the north of Valparaiso is Viña del Mar, Chile's answer to the French and Italian Riviera. Here can be found the well-maintained sandy beaches overlooked by luxurious seaside hotels and condominiums, expensive restaurants and night clubs, and the country's only casino. Viña is the main tourist centre during the Chilean summer, with crowds of people enjoying all of the typical seaside resort activities including swimming, boating, sunbathing, paragliding, and people watching. Compared to the rest of the country, the city has clearly benefited from significant foreign investment, although it may not be to your taste. To me, the city seems to be trying too hard to be something else, to emulate a European resort, but not quite hitting the mark. It can be too populated, too noisy, and too busy, with too much traffic crawling along the one seaside road through the city.

Approximately 45 minutes south of Valparaiso is the small village of Isla Negra, one of Pablo Neruda's three homes, all of which are now owned and managed by the Pablo Neruda Foundation and open to the public with displays documenting the life and work of Chile's most famous citizen. The first, *La Chascona*, is situated on the side of a steep hillside street in the Barrio Bellavista section of Santiago, while the second, *La Sebastiana,* can be found on an even steeper hillside in

Valparaiso. *Isla Negra*, reputed to be Neruda's favorite residence, is located on an oceanfront property that he shared with his third wife Matilde Urrutia. He and Matilde are buried on the property, side by side, looking out together over Neruda's beloved Pacific Ocean.

Isla Negra is not in fact an island, nor is it black. The house is named after a dark outcrop of rock visible from the property just off the sandy beach below the house. The property was purchased by Neruda in 1937 on his return from Europe as a place where he could work on his Canto General, the well-regarded poems he composed on the history, nature and struggles of the South American people. "The wild seashore of Isla Negra, with the tumultuous movements of the ocean, allowed me to passionately get involved in the labour of my new Canto" he wrote in his memoires.

The house, built around an original stone tower constructed on the sea cliff, is shaped to resemble a ship with low ceilings, dark wooden floors and narrow hallways. Over time, Neruda added a series of rooms, with the house being completed in 1945. My favorite room is Neruda's "writing room", covered by a tin roof so the author could hear the rain while he gazed out over his ocean views.

A tour of Isla Negra, and indeed all of Neruda's homes, is a must for every visitor to Chile. His influence on the country and its people cannot be underestimated, and by learning more about the author, his life and his works, one is provided with significant insight into the cultural and societal backbone of this wonderful country.

In addition to its eccentric architecture, Isla Negra provides a view into Neruda's passion for collecting. He appears to have picked up everything, and more specifically, anything to do with the sea. The house is filled with collections of sea shells, ships in bottles, carved native masks, numerous and massive ship's figureheads, a part of his extensive library, an impressive narwhale tusk, as well as his large collection of beetles and butterflies. Every wall, table, desk, hallway and room is covered with his unique and eccentric collections. One room with a large picture window facing the ocean was set up as a bar or tavern in which Nerdua loved to entertain his guests. He did enjoy his wine and hard spirits, and the stories of his alcoholic excesses are legendary.

CHAPTER EIGHT
SANTIAGO'S
YELLOW DEATH

astillo Verde is located in the town of San Juan de Pirque, adjacent to the village of La Puntilla and the larger town of Pirque proper. All are connected by a two-lane road in various states of repair that winds along the south bank of the Maipo River. The river valley, called *el Cajon del Maipo*, is very popular as a weekend escape for city residents to enjoy such activities as hiking, rock climbing, horseback riding, kayaking and river rafting, then recovering with a soak in one of the many natural mineral hot springs in the area, followed by a leisurely meal in the numerous excellent restaurants along the valley.

Fridays are very busy days as families, couples and adventurous singles drive, ride their bikes or hike up the *cajon* to enjoy the great outdoors. Should the weather be fine on Sunday, the road back to the city can become a traffic nightmare with gridlock lasting well into the night. What would be frustrating to a North American forced to endure a long drive home from a holiday weekend is taken in stride by Chileans who use this free time in their vehicles to chat with family, catch some sleep, or try to recover from too much sun and too much fun.

San Juan de Pirque sits at approximately 1,200 meters above sea level, about 700 meters above and to the south-east of the city of Greater Santiago. The drive from Castillo Verde to Central Santiago takes between 40 minutes to an hour and a half, depending on traffic, but the change is profound as one travels from a largely rural area of great natural beauty into one of the most modern and sophisticated cities in the world.

Greater Santiago, according to the latest census, is home to approximately 6.5 million people, all of whom live within 642 square kilometers in a bowl-shaped valley surrounded by mountains. With the Andes to the east, the Chilean coastal range to the west, the *Cordon de Chacabuco* to the north and the *Angostura de Paine* to the south, the panorama on a clear day is breathtaking as snow capped peaks, including the 6,600 meter high Tupungato volcano and the 5,400 meter high Cerro El Plomo mountain, are visible throughout the city. The oldest sections of the city are essentially on an island as the Mapocho River splits into two branches to the north, rejoining a few miles to the south, with residential suburbs beginning to encroach on the beginning of the mountain slopes as they rise to the east above the city.

Originally founded in 1541 by the Spanish conquistador Pedro de Valdivia, the city grew and adapted to the rapidly changing face of Chile. The location was originally chosen for its moderate climate, superb agricultural potential, and the ease with which it could be defended from attacks by the local Arauco Indians, who were not very pleased to see the Spanish invade their lands. The city was in fact destroyed later that same year as the Arauco, under their leader Michimalonco, drove the Spanish out. But the Spanish came back, and it was not until the 1880's that the Araucanian Indians were completely defeated and subjugated. A fictionalized story of Santiago's early days can be found in Isabel Allende's illuminating novel *Ines of My Soul*.

The city grew slowly through the 19th century, and it was not until the late 1800's that the nitrate boom in the north brought prosperity and development to the Santiago region. Through the early decades of the 20th century, Santiago began its transformation into a modern city as migration from the south and the north, as well as from other South American countries, significantly increased the city's population. Over the last twenty years, strong economic growth has led to Santiago becoming one of Latin America's most modern metropolitan areas with extensive urban development, fine dining and shopping, beautiful public art installations, modern architecture, and the beginning of a rejuvenation of the much older downtown neighbourhoods.

Today Santiago, and, indeed, Chile, is one of South America's most stable and prosperous regions. It leads Latin America in competitiveness, quality of life, political stability and economic freedom with lower corruption and poverty rates than any other nation on the continent. Its press is relatively free, with strong human and democratic development standards. It also has the largest gross domestic product per capita in all of South America.

Architecture is an important and prestigious discipline in Chile, and its prominence can be seen and experienced throughout Santiago. I have been told there are more professional architects per capita in Chile than anywhere else in the world. With this plethora of talent, the well-developed centre of the city, home to familiar international companies as well as local banks, businesses and a new and growing group of entrepreneurs, is comprised of highly original and beautiful office and condominium towers, with each property prominently displaying the name of the its architect and builder. I wonder why other cities have not adopted this practice? As you walk at street level, you look up to see these original and unique buildings, and at the same time you can learn who designed them, and who built them. The designers and builders take great pride in their accomplishments, and are proud to display their names on their projects.

As in most large cities, Santiago is known by its neighbourhoods. Gran Santiago is in fact made up of 32 *comunas*, or boroughs, each separately governed and each imposing its own set of taxes, fees and regulations on its residents. It was in one of these *comunas* that I was required to purchase a license for my vehicle.

The origins of these *comunas* extend back to the historic beginnings of the city, and for many serve to segregate Santiago's residents by the class and economic divisions that still exist today. For example, Providencia, Vitacura and Las Condes, three of the city's more affluent *comunas*, are home to modern office towers, expensive condominiums, and large stately mansions, as well as the latest shops and fashionable restaurants. *Recoleta*, a growing residential neighborhood moving up into the foothills of the Andes to the east of the city, has become home to Santiago's wealthy in their large estates with their extensive and well-kept gardens. Bellavista has evolved into a key centre for Santiago nightlife, as clubs and restaurants cater to young and old alike.

More interesting to me are some of the older sections of the city, once home to the Santiago elite, but for decades having falling into disrepair, disrepute, and, in some sections, a certain lawlessness. Fortunately, as Chile's economy has prospered, increasing numbers of people are returning to these older neighbourhoods, restoring and transforming the mature and architecturally fascinating buildings into homes, condos and lofts with significant character. In the past, wealthier and more "upper class" Chileans would never cross into these older *comunas* the other side of Plaza Italia, a central demarcation point between the more modern sections of the city and its much older neighbourhoods. Today, tourists and residents alike flock to *Barrio Brasil,* the area around the beautiful parks surrounding *Cerro Santa Lucia,* and *Barrio Lastarria.*

To me, one of the most fascinating sections of the old city is *Barrio Yungay,* a wonderful, mostly residential neighbourhood to the west of central Santiago. It is seldom mentioned in any of the popular guide books, but is a treasure to visit if you want to experience the renaissance that is occurring within many of these ancient and once abandoned residential *barrios.*

Barrio Yungay includes the 40 hectare *Parque Quinta Normal,* the city's first botanical garden. Created in 1841, the park began as a small field with a school dedicated to experimenting with new agricultural techniques and the development of plant and crop strains that could be adapted to Chile's climate. Now the park provides Santiago residents with playgrounds, soccer fields, tennis courts and bathing pools, as well as a number of public and private museums.

In the centre of the B*arrio Yungay* sits the *Peluqueria Francesa.* Founded in 1868, and moved to its present location in 1925, you can have your hair cut or a hot shave done with a straight razor, strop and cream whipped up in a bowl, then move upstairs to enjoy a fabulous lunch or dinner starting with a wide range of pisco concoctions or accompanied by excellent Chilean wines, while at the same time purchasing some of the many antiques available throughout the restaurant, including, if you so desire, the table and chairs at which you are seated. You can have your car parked by a valet service run by Pedro, who will also, for a small fee, repair that antique lamp you just purchased during your meal.

Across the street from the *Peluqueria Francesa* is the *Eglisia de la Preciosa Sangre,* or Church of the Blessed Blood. I am not a Catholic, but you have to love the great names they come up with for their places of worship. The Church is quite an imposing building with a large dome peering over the top of the *barrio*. Construction of the Church began in 1873, finishing in 1906, and it was originally used as a cloister for aristocratic single mothers who needed to hide out during their pregnancy, so-called "rebellious" women needing to hide from their husbands because of their outspokenness, and other women who were deemed to suffer from mental issues – most likely another name for "rebelliousness". One of the more famous inmates in the cloister was Theresa Wilms Montt who escaped the Church with the help of another famous Chilean poet, Vincent Huidobro.

Vincent once lived in a house situated on a tiny but gorgeous square in the middle of nearby *Barrio Conha y Toro*. The building has since been transformed into one of the city's finer restaurants, Zully, facing a beautiful stone fountain around which the *barrio's* residents gather to meet, talk and gossip. Every day fresh rose petals are scattered on the restaurant's stone steps leading up into the very hip and interestingly-decorated dining rooms, most of which are small, intimate, and face into a gardened interior courtyard with a bubbling water feature. There is also a rooftop terrace with stunning views of the city skyline. Strangely, the establishment is owned by Joe Westrate, a native of Kalamazoo Michigan, who has decorated the walls of this traditional Chilean establishment with pictures of his favorite home state sports teams, including the Vikings, the Red Wings, the Pistons, and numerous photographs of the Michigan Wolverines college teams. Despite the unorthodox decorations, the cuisine is inventive and tasteful, providing an alternative view of many traditional Chilean dishes.

Just down the street and around the corner from the *Peluquria* is *Pasaje Adirana Cousiño*, one of my favorite residential streets in all of Santiago. It is only open to walkers as, in the middle of the two large tiled sidewalks, is a long garden filled with fragrant flowers, blossoming trees, Chilean palms and native grasses. The century-old two and three storey houses are painted differing hues of warm colours, with wooden doors providing glimpses into gardened interior courtyards and paneled rooms filled with antique furniture. Children and their nannies play on the walkways, teenagers kiss in doorways, and walking peacefully down the short boulevard one hears little of the city's noise or bustle. It is rumoured that one of Santiago's more famous and prestigious architects lives in a large house on the street's corner, an indication of the beginning of this wonderful *barrio's* imminent revival.

Travelling to and from *Barrio* Yungay, and indeed throughout Santiago, is easily managed by the city's modern and efficient transportation system. The major highways that bisect and surround Santiago are almost all toll roads, and it seems to be a bit of a game for drivers to try and beat this system and save a few pesos. On our first trips to the country we were picked up by various friends or taken to Pirque by our faithful taxi driver Don Alejandro. Almost everyone had a different route to take, and I am sure each decision was made trying to dodge the tolls, small as they may be.

Taxis are very available and very affordable throughout the city. They also do not accept tips, unless you are a stupid gringo like me and clearly don't understand the local currency. There are also numerous *collectivos*, taxis that drive around a prescribed route all day picking up and dropping off passengers. These are the least expensive and most efficient means of getting around if you are familiar with a route, and as long as you don't mind sharing the car with a large family, a kissing couple, or a stern grandmother disapproving of your clothing choice and lack of Spanish.

One of the drawbacks to Santiago's location, and the spectacular mountains that surround it, is the ever-present evil of pollution. The city is one of the more smog bound in South America as, sitting in a bowl, it is hard for exhaust, smoke and other emissions to escape. Over the years many different solutions have been proposed to improve the air quality, including one suggestion by a Japanese engineering firm, turned down by the city, to blow up a section of the Andes Mountains nearest the city to allow the pollution to escape. As we sit high above and to the east of the city at Castillo Verde, on a bad day we can see the pall that sits over the city, and these bad days are numerous, especially in the summer months.

In an attempt to reduce the pollution, in 2005 the city initiated a five-year program to replace all of the diesel-fuelled buses with natural gas vehicles. At the same time, they wanted to reduce what the bureaucrats saw as confusion and congestion by transitioning from the existing system of over 3,000 privately-owned and operated transportation companies to a more streamlined organization of surface transit managed by only ten much larger, well-financed entities. In our short few years in Chile, we have watched the transition of this transportation system with great interest and, I must admit, some humour.

During our first trips to Santiago the streets were full of hundreds of small yellow buses that careened in and out of traffic to pick up or deposit commuters. Called "yellow death", the drivers of these buses appeared to consider the safety and convenience of their passengers, other vehicles, and the general public as secondary to getting to the next destination as quickly as possible. It was a brave pedestrian who would venture out in front of one of these buses, and often they only slowed down rather than stop to drop off or pick up a rider,

We were also mystified as to how anyone recognized which bus to take, or how much to pay. There was no central organized fare regime or standard route map, and travelers seemed to pay different amounts as they climbed aboard. There were also no apparent designated stops, no order to the chaos, and each bus was covered in signs with the names of specific streets, *comunas*, districts, neighborhoods, and even stores and shopping centres as their destinations, none of which could be found on a map and whose location seemed intuitively known only to customers of a specific bus driver. To catch a bus, you had to wander out into traffic and flag one down. Often you would see a forlorn commuter dodge into the street only to wave down the wrong bus, much to the annoyance of the driver who, it appeared, took out his anger by swerving to try and run down the mistaken pedestrian.

The multitude of signs on these buses was accompanied by many other more personal decorations, including flags, statues, family pictures, as well as Madonnas, crucifixes, communion beads and other spiritual paraphernalia. The religious tone to these bus decorations was not only an indication of the importance of God and His Son in Chile – almost 69% of the population identified themselves as Catholic in the last census, with another 13% calling themselves Evangelical Protestants – but also a clear prayer for the well being of the vehicle's crowds of passengers and those unfortunate souls who might step into its path.

And as these hordes of yellow death buses wove in and out of traffic, they announced their routes with blaring horns in various tones and songs while belching out plumes of black, oily smoke. It was rumoured that, because the old buses' days were numbered during the transition to more efficient natural gas fueled vehicles, their owners simply stopped maintaining the engines and exhaust systems, resulting in even worse emissions and city-wide pollution. I also wonder where all the old buses have gone? There were supposed to be over 7,000 of these ancient vehicles, and the graveyard for their corpses must be quite something.

Over the next few years as the "yellow death" buses were retired and newer, larger, more fuel efficient and environmentally friendly vehicles travelled the streets of Santiago, the backlash was enormous. Poor communication resulted in most passengers not knowing which bus to take, and a cashless system required passes or fare tickets to be purchased in advance at designated kiosks, offices or over the Internet. The confusion was compounded by the fact that the number of buses declined by more than half, supposedly to eliminate the route redundancy in the old system. But with the route changes and new time schedules, people did not understand where to go, how to get there, or how much to pay. It was chaos on the streets.

The ensuing scandal is rumored to have forced the resignation of a few high-ranking government officials, and the current President Bachelet has been fighting a rear-guard action to try and recover what small amount of good will remains in this well-meaning attempt to control pollution. To make matters worse, many of the old yellow diesel-fuel buses have been disguised the same green colour as the new Transantiago vehicles and have reappeared on the city streets, careening around the new transit system in an attempt to pirate passengers and dodge their enforced retirement. Over time I am sure the city will achieve its stated goals, but there will be significant trial and tribulation to get there.

The other very apparent aspect of Chilean life, most visible in Santiago, is the high level of income inequality that exists. While there is obvious wealth in the country, this prosperity exists beside significant and widespread poverty. The streets are crowded with new cars, the sidewalks and stores full of the latest fashions and consumer goods, but those same streets, sidewalks and storefronts are kept clean by a huge army of the poor looking for a few pesos for their work. When you park your car, someone will always appear to guide you in to your spot and direct you out, all for a bit of money. They often wear an official-looking uniform, although no such formal job exists, and many will offer to wash your car while you are shopping. Store fronts and sidewalks are swept and raked without being asked, with the worker then asking for payment.

As you walk along the street, you can find any number of people with elaborate blankets spread out on the sidewalks selling sunglasses, books, toys, trinkets, bootleg videos, food, coffee, vegetables, indeed almost anything. The blankets are bordered by long strings that are used to quickly bundle the contraband goods out of sight when the police appear. Although such trading activities are illegal, the *Carabineros* tend to turn a blind eye to most of these street vendors. And while you are waiting in your car for a stoplight to change, you may be entertained by a juggler or gymnast performing tricks for donations, as well as people selling everything from newspapers, candy, ice cream, drinks, olives, avocados and other fresh produce. It is also very well organized, with olives, for example, being sold at one street light and avocados at the next. Marcela tells us she does most of her shopping while driving home, and I can certainly see how this can be accomplished.

Yet despite the wide disparity in income levels, and a very large impoverished population, you seldom see any begging or what we North American's would designate as homeless people. If someone asks you for money, it will be for some service or product – seldom will you simply be asked for your spare change. An illuminating example occurred when I was walking near the banking district in downtown Santiago. A reasonably well-dressed young man approached me and, as I understood him in my rudimentary Spanish, offered something to me for sale. I shook my head and kept walking. Following beside me, he smiled and asked if I spoke English, then where I was from, and other friendly questions. Feeling in no danger, I entered into a conversation as his English was quite good.

After our introductions and small talk, he explained that he was a university student trying to pay his way through school by selling his poems. Poets are revered in Chile, and many take this up as a full-time occupation. This young man was studying literature and wanted to be a poet. I was impressed, and offered a ten thousand-peso note – about $20 – for one of his poems. The man was ecstatic, thanked me profusely, and presented me with a small, photocopied paper with a decorative border printed with one of his own poems. We then parted company, me feeling very self-righteous and the student pocketing probably the largest amount he had ever received for his work. Unfortunately, as I learned later when it was translated, it was not a very good poem.

Returning home one night after experiencing but not understanding a movie at a local cinema, we were waiting for a light to change on a main road. While stopped for the brief one or two minutes it took for the signal to turn green, we had our windows cleaned with fresh, soapy water (not the dirty squeegees we see in the North) by a well-dressed gentleman, were entertained by a young man juggling four bright, burning torches being thrown up in the air and around his body (he did display some burns on his hands when we paid him), and offered rich, dark, hot coffee by a man with a large caldron on his back attached to a hose and nozzle from which he poured his beverages into clean cups. He looked like one of the flame-throwing soldiers we had seen in the movie. None begged or asked for money, they simply took our payments, when offered, with dignity and thanks.

Movie theatres in Chile are very similar to those in North America. The majority have been transformed into multiplex establishments showing a number of movies at one time. The décor, refreshment stands and displays are the same as those we find everywhere else, a bit of a disappointment, really. Yet the Chile factor always works its way even into the running of these businesses. With a scheduled start time of 7.30 pm, we were first lined up in the hallway, and could only enter the theater at just after 8.00 pm, a half an hour late. The Chilean disrespect for time schedules was ever present.

The movies available are, for the most part, all North American blockbusters, and they seem to favour loud, action-packed adventure and super-hero films. Many are subtitled in Spanish with the original English soundtrack, but increasingly movies in Chile are dubbed into Spanish. Unfortunately, it appears the film companies use the same people to dub these movies, and often each voice can take on a few different characters in the same movie. If you enjoy this form of entertainment, you will hear the same person portraying many different actors whose true voices are familiar to English speakers who attend the cinema. It is odd to hear the same voice come out of Jack Nicholson's mouth as for Arnold Schwarzenegger or Michael Caine. Gone are the nuance of native accents and speech patterns in these dubbed versions.

There is also a thriving black market in bootleg movies. Whenever the latest film opens in theaters, the next day you can purchase pirated copies on the streets of Santiago for less than the cost of a ticket to see the film at the cinema. Many of these bootleg copies are digitally transferred directly from the movie house projector, but a large portion are made by hand. A man beside us at one blockbuster opening night was clearly filming the movie with his hand-held video recorder. If you don't mind the sound of people coughing, the occasional loss of picture as a patron blocks the camera or the cameraman dips down behind the seat when security sticks their head into the room, it's one way to watch a new film in the comfort of your home. Just don't let the *carabineros* catch you with a copy.

Another reason Chileans attend the cinema is the opportunity to be with their significant other away from the restrictive oversight of parents and chaperones. In a society so dominated by the Catholic Church, young Chilean couples love to kiss. In any outdoor park, bench, bus shelter, anywhere and everywhere, you will see young couples locked in an embrace, their lips together. Kissing goes on everywhere, and it is quite wonderful.

I suppose one reason for so much public kissing is that these young couples have no where to go to be alone. Their homes are full of brothers and sisters, grandparents, as well as parents who would not allow such behaviour in their presence. The kids don't seem to mind displaying their affection in public, and I suppose it is also a means of birth control – if adolescents did find some privacy, the birthrate in a country that frowns on contraception might be much higher than it already is. Movies are another venue where kissing is rampant, and while I did see a few coats conspicuously covering laps as couples watched their films, there was no opportunity for young men to realistically pass first base with their significant other. I am also quite sure that, despite their passionate embraces, those kissing still understood more of the movie than I did.

CHAPTER NINE
CARLITO'S WAY

On another of our trips to experience the late Chilean spring, Pancho and Angela, along with their children Manuel and Violeta, piled us into their jeep to have lunch with Carlito, a friend who lived with his extended family high up in the Colorado River Valley, a canyon that flowed into the Maipo.

Carlos Arenas, or Carlito to his friends, is descended from a long line of proud and productive *inquilinos*, people who worked the land for the owners of large haciendas since the time Chile was colonized by the Spanish in the early 1500's. Hacienda Colorado was one of the largest in the country, occupying steep river valleys and pastures stretching from the Maipo River north to Portillo. It encompassed thousands and thousands of square kilometers of breathtaking beauty on which were raised sheep, goats, cattle and horses. The *inquilinos* and their families lived on the land, herding the animals under their care on horseback throughout the spring, summer and fall months which extended generally from early October through to late April.

During the land reform years under Salvador Allende's government, Hacienda Colorado was broken up into smaller tracts of land with many of these being given to the *inquilinos*, along with the animals on the property. There were also rumours that the owners of the Hacienda lost much of their property to gambling debts. However, with the Pinochet coup in 1973, the entire area was appropriated by the government and the *inquilinos* thrown off their properties. The government worried about a possible war with Argentina, and the old Hacienda lands were perfect for secret incursions across the Andes into Chile. In addition, the fast flowing Colorado River had become a key source of hydroelectric power for Santiago, and the dictatorship did not want a bunch of opposition leftists roaming about the hills disrupting the capital's power grid. The *inquilinos* were intimately familiar with all of the ways one could travel through and hide in the mountains, and the junta did not want them freely disseminating this knowledge.

Pinochet's concerns about the area proved to be quite prescient as an almost successful assassination attempt by a group of leftist guerillas occurred on the main highway through the Maipo Canyon just down from the Colorado River. Interestingly, on eBay you can purchase the purported windshield from the General's car, complete with bullet holes from that attack. I wonder how many of these windshields are sold each year to gullible collectors?

With the installation of military control over the Colorado River Valley, a large army base was commissioned at its entrance and an armed checkpoint constructed. No one could enter the canyon unless they first passed though this checkpoint. Among those who were gradually permitted access to the area following the Pinochet years were the former *inquilinos* who had grazed their animals and made their livelihood on the land. Carlito's father was one of the first to return with his sheep, goats and cows, and today Carlito has continued in his footsteps.

The only others allowed to pass the checkpoint are those who can prove they own animals that are grazing on the hillsides. In a stroke of genius, Pancho purchased a small number of sheep and goats and gave them to Carlito to raise. With an official document stating he owned animals being husbanded in the valleys, he was allowed access, and we were permitted to accompany him, after some serious review of our passports and other documents by the guards at the checkpoint.

Carlito and his extended family spend their summer months high up in the Andes within walking distance of the river. Shelter is provided by rough tin and wood-framed buildings, reassembled each year on the return from the winter and heavy, deep snows that blanket the region. When we visited, Carlito, his wife and children, his mother, brothers and sisters, along with their own families, were enjoying their freedom among a cacophony of baby goats and sheep, cows, chickens, pigs, horses and, of course, about a million dogs. There are a lot of dogs in Chile.

We brought presents of candies and soft drinks for the children, and a new sombrero for Carlito. In return, he killed one of his lambs and slowly cooked it for us for lunch. Called an *asado* in Chile, meat is cooked over an open log fire, either directly over the coals, or, in the case of the lamb, vertically splayed on sticks stuck in the ground beside the fire. The meal was accompanied by some of the best goat cheese I have eaten, prepared by Carlito's family, and numerous bottles of fine Chilean red wine. Fresh tomatoes, onions, cucumbers and celery were also served. Chileans normally don't like their vegetables to touch each other and are usually found in separate piles on their plates. They looked quite strangely at me as I combined them all together into what we gringos would call a salad.

It was a delicious meal, made more so by being afforded the stunning views of the Andes, condors flying overhead, the noise of the livestock and dogs around us, the babbling mountain stream beside us, and the hot sun. Before long, everyone had taken their ponchos and, using them as blankets, stretched out for a siesta.

The Chilean Andes are one of the most seismically active regions in the world. Situated on the so-called "ring of fire" along the Pacific Ocean, the country is home to more than 2,000 volcanoes, of which experts say over 500 are potentially active. About sixty of these have erupted over the past four centuries, with some spectacular explosions and lava flows. Fortunately, most of these more active sites are situated far to the south or the north of Castillo Verde, although there is one very large and, to date, dormant volcano located up the valley from our house.

One of the only benefits of this seismic activity is the abundance of hot springs, called *thermas*, found throughout the mountains. Many of these *thermas* have become tourist destinations with hotels, spas and other activities, but most are simple pools of mineral water bubbling out of the mountainside.

On the drive back from Carlito's we decided we should refresh ourselves by dipping into one of the many natural and undeveloped hot springs that are found throughout the mountains. The pool in question, in addition to the rejuvenating properties of hot mineral immersion, provided the added benefit of additional healthy minerals that were infused in its mud, and as you sat in the hot water, you were supposed to cover your exposed skin with this mud pack and let it remain in place until it dried. We looked quite something sitting there in our bathing suits, sun glasses and hats, covered in a dark, smelly mud. I am not sure I will ever get the smell or the grit totally out of my clothing.

Sitting in the heat and mud, I could not fail to notice the display of crosses planted in the ground just above our pool. They were decorated with coloured ribbons, and candles had been recently burned around them. I asked what they represented, and was told that a group of six young people had been recently killed by a rock slide as they lounged in this same pool. I asked if we could leave soon.

Sitting in the hot and steamy pool, I thought again about some of the other interesting and challenging hurdles we had overcome in buying Castillo Verde. One of the more confusing aspects of acquiring property in Chile is the use of different currencies and monetary units, and more particularly the existence of the *Unidad de Fomento*, or UF. You see this nomenclature everywhere in Chile, especially where new housing developments, condos or apartments are being advertised with their accompanying price stated in UF. What was this strange currency? There were no bills or coins saying they were UF and, when asked, I was told its value changes every day. Great, I would need a calculator to determine what things were worth. And to further complicate matters, we were also constantly translating the Chilean peso into both Canadian and US currencies.

The *Unidad de Fomento*, or UF, was created in January 1967 to account for inflation in the price of major items like housing and vehicles, as well as all bank loans and any longer-term fixed payments such as salaries or the retaining of a lawyer or other advisor on a monthly basis. In essence the UF is an inflation index, and the exchange rate between the peso and the UF is adjusted daily so that the value of the UF remains constant.

For example, let's assume we had agreed to pay Carlos 150 million pesos for Castillo Verde in March 2005. At the time, using the appropriate exchange rate of 1 UF = 30,186 pesos, the value of our house was approximately 496.919 UF. Annual inflation rates in Chile had been running at between 3% and 4% for some time, but recently had climbed closer to 7%. As a result, the value of a UF climbed significantly, and stood at 32.724 pesos when we actually closed the purchase in July 2007. If we had agreed to pay Carlos in UF when we originally shook hands, we would have had to pay him 162.6 million pesos at closing. As you can see, Carlos would have been protected from the negative impact of inflation. Fortunately for us, we did not convert the agreed-upon price in pesos into UF until we actually closed the sale in July 2007.

However, the impact of the UF does not end there. Any mortgage or bank loan you acquire is also converted into UF, and so are your payments. Thus, while the loan value in pesos may climb due to the inflationary impact on the UF conversion, one hopes the monthly payments will help to counteract the increase in the loan value.

I don't think Carlito has ever had to worry about the UF conversion price, and as I climbed out of the hot spring and drove away from the idyllic mountain valley in which he lived, I wondered who was the smarter, or the happier.

CHAPTER TEN

THE NOBLE CHILEAN HORSE

n addition to the vast numbers of dogs in Chile, horses are a way of life throughout the country and are found everywhere. Not a day goes by at Castillo Verde that you don't hear the sound of a horse and rider moving sedately past the house. The clip-clop sound of hooves has become a unique and familiar sound, serving as a constant reminder that we are not in Kansas any more.

One day Pancho asked if I would like to take a short ride into the hills to view some spectacular scenery and experience how many Chileans spend their holidays. I explained that I had never been on a horse before, and in fact was not really sure which end was the front. Pancho assured me that his horses – he had six at the time – were gentle, well-trained, and all I needed to do was trust the horse and give him his head to take me safely on our route.

Now after spending many, many weeks with Pancho and his family, I knew that all of these so-called gentle and tame horses spend most of their time roaming the vast expanses of mountainside surrounding his property. Days could go by without anyone sitting on them, much less an inexperienced, overweight and slightly paranoid gringo from Canada. Frequently Pancho, Angela and their family will take three to six week long treks into the mountains on horseback, along with their tents, food, sleeping bags and other supplies carried on additional horses. Similar to the North American practice of hiking in the mountains or canoeing across lakes, these treks by horse are a popular pastime in Chile. However, it can be months between times that these horses have experienced a rider on their backs, and I was concerned that a novice rider would not be very welcome after an extensive period of freedom roaming the mountain pastures.

The horse for my inaugural ride was named Buen Amigo, fortunately one of his gentlest, and the horse Pancho's six-year old daughter rode when they took their extended family trips into the Andes. After being shown a few rudimentary skills, such as how to start, stop and turn, off we went.

The first few hours were quite enjoyable. I sat comfortably on the Chilean saddle, a series of blankets and sheepskins covering a small wooden frame, with the reins loosely held in my hands. Buen Amigo ambled slowly along, seeming to know where we were going and how to get there. She was a pleasure for a first time rider, and I thought I was grasping the skills, feeling confident, and that maybe my fear of these huge animals and their tiny brains was unfounded.

Then we started to climb. As we moved above the treeline, our route consisted of a series of steep switchbacks up a mountainside composed of loose shale, stones and boulders. The horse's hooves often slipped, sending my heart racing as I looked down quite sheer cliffs that would certainly end my days if the horse were to stumble or I was to fall. I held on, as instructed, with my knees and thighs, and after a while the saddle started to become decidedly less comfortable. But the views were amazing, and as we climbed higher the vast expanse of the snow-covered Andes gradually began to appear over the summit we were approaching.

Finally, after about four hours of riding, we reached the ridge Pancho had targeted as our destination. We dismounted for a lovely lunch of sliced meats, cheeses, bread, fruit, and, of course, wine. It is traditional on these horse treks to drink your wine from a cow's horn, and I enjoyed the experience of drinking the robust reds and then sinking the pointed end of the horn into the ground while I chewed off another bite of bread and dried beef, gazing out over majestic mountains as far as the eye could see. Pancho pointed out some of the key peaks, places he had traveled by horseback, and we then laid back on our ponchos, tilted our hats over our eyes, and had a brief siesta. I would need it.

Going up, it appeared, is a lot easier than going down. Like hiking, ascending is less strenuous on your legs than descending a steep mountainside. In addition to the wear on your thighs and knees, the added force of gravity requires that you increase your effort. It was the same for Buen Amigo, my trusted horse. In descending on horseback, you also have to sit much further back in the saddle with a straight spine, and hold on much tighter with your thighs. The prior consumption of a few cow's horns full of strong red wine did not help in the effort.

The descent also involved more slips and stumbles as the shale and rocks seemed to slide out from under Buen Amigo's hooves with terrifying regularity. Pancho, with a look of concern on his face, told me to hold on and to trust the horse. He told me he had not lost anyone on these rides, and that I should not worry. This was wonderful news! He had not lost anyone! I failed to inquire how many were still in hospital recuperating from their injuries.

As we finally re-entered the tree line, we arrived at a creek we had to cross, a task that had been accomplished with little trouble on the ascent. We dismounted for a brief swim in the cold fresh mountain water, and then prepared to move on. However, Buen Amigo wanted to start before I was fully seated in my saddle. With one leg in the stirrup, and the rest of me holding on for dear life, Buen Amigo deftly and quickly hopped across some rocks and the stream, dragging me along for the ride. My shoulder was wrenched, and a few cuts were sustained as I banged into rocks and a few thick, unyielding tree branches. Fortunately nothing more serious occurred, and after Pancho corralled Buen Amigo, I mounted properly and we continued on our way.

Another fact I learned about horses is they like to get home as quickly as possible. They can be slow and steady on the way out, but when they sense they are nearing their stable, and in my case the opportunity to remove the inexperienced, heavy gringo off their back and get something to eat, they tend to speed up and ignore much of what the rider wants them to do. I had not been given any pointers on how to manage a horse in a canter, gallop or anything other than a slow walk, and when Buen Amigo took off for home, I was bounced along, again holding on for dear life to whatever I could grab while trying to dodge the tree branches that my horse so easily avoided.

Once safely back at Pancho's I looked at my watch and realized we had been out for just over nine hours – so much for "a short ride in the country to view some scenery". My face was burnt, my arms and legs cut from branches, my knees ached and the calves of both my legs were bruised and bleeding from clenching and rubbing the horse's flanks.

As in most outdoor pursuits, I realized that proper gear was necessary, and a few days later Pancho proudly presented me with my own pair of *botas*, think hand-made pigskin chaps that covered the leg from the knee down, as well as a set of beautiful sliver spurs. The *botas* protect your legs from branches, while also cushioning your calves from the horse's flanks and the saddle cinches that can cut into your leg. I have used them many times since, and riding has become much more enjoyable. The spurs, however, await a day when I believe I will have sufficient skill to use them.

During this first ride, we encountered a number of *huasos*, the Chilean counterpart to the cowboy, who ride the hills working their herds of cows, goats, sheep and horses. Carlito was a true *huaso*, and so are the many men on horseback who ride past Castillo Verde.

The Chilean *huaso* is recognized by their distinct clothing and equipment – a wide, flat-brimmed straw or felt sombrero, a short but colourful pancho, *botas* over well polished ankle-length boots, and bright silver spurs. The saddle stirrups are normally made from wood, and are richly carved with designs that date back centuries. The *huasos* are a handsome group, riding upright with proud demeanor and true skill as they work their mounts daily in what can, as I discovered, be quite treacherous terrain.

The culmination of a *huaso's* skill is found at the many Chilean rodeos that occur around the country. There is no more perfect indicator of the importance of the horse to this country than the popularity of rodeo. Second only to football as a spectator sport, or soccer as we North Americans call it, rodeo draws thousands to its unique, circular *medialuna* riding rings every year. The main rodeo season is held between the months of August and May, with approximately 350 accredited events culminating in the National Championships held at Rancagua, a city about 150 kilometers south of Santiago.

Chilean rodeo is quite different to what we find under the same name in North America. Gone are the displays of speed and recklessness as wagons or horses race against time around barrels, the violent roping and throwing down of animals, or the riding of distressed bucking broncos. In Chile, animals are more respected and are seldom harmed in rodeo.

In Chile, the word "rodeo" originally designated a time when the animals up in the hills were rounded up at the start of winter and driven down the mountains to the warmer and more protected valleys where they were sorted and branded in unique corrals defined by rough stone walls. This almost ritualized form of livestock management evolved into the sport and spectacle of today's competitive Chilean rodeo. It is a demonstration of pure equestrian skill and experience, almost ballet-like in its movement, as a team of two horses and riders earn points by moving a steer through a series of pre-determined maneuvers and pinning the animal motionless three times in designated and well-padded zones located around the outside edge of the competition ring.

It is beautiful to see, and no where else can you experience the skill and dexterity of a horse in such close communication with its rider. While there are a number of *huasos* who are professional rodeo participants with sponsorships and endorsements to support them, the vast majority of rodeo competitors are ordinary working people who, when not at the rodeo, are in the mountains earning a living with their livestock.

Rodeo participants can only use purebred Chilean horses, a unique breed that has evolved from the first horses introduced to the country by Spanish soldiers in the early 1500's. Brought originally from Peru by the conquistador Pedro de Valdivia in 1541, these horses originally came to South America from the West Indies, principally from the islands of Cuba and Santo Domingo. Only the strongest and hardiest of horses could survive in Chile as the perils of harsh weather, droughts, floods and rough terrain were compounded by a soldier's need for dependability in long travel and fighting.

Over the centuries the Chilean horse adapted its organs, limbs and senses to this new environment, defining the unique breed that exists today. In 1893 the purity of the Chilean horse was established with the *Stud Book de la Raza Chilena* (sic) that published certified registries of the horse's genealogy. Then, in 1910, the *Sociedad Nacional de Agricultura* created the "Selection for Registry of the Chilean Horse" establishing definitive standards for the full development of the breed. All of Pancho's horses are pure bred Chilean horses, and he will have no other.

It was one of these classic horses that I had the privilege to ride in Chile, and I was exceedingly happy, as I looked down the sheer cliffs on which we were perched, that I was astride more than 500 years of horse evolution familiar with this terrain.

CHAPTER ELEVEN

I LEARN MY BRAIN IS MADE OF TEFLON

As the complications of buying, owning and renovating a home in a foreign country began to mount up, it became very apparent that we would need to learn the Spanish language. We began our education with some beginner courses back in Canada where I quickly discovered that at some point my brain matter had been transformed into teflon – everything I tried to remember just slipped out of my memory into some heretofore unknown part of my cranium. It was most frustrating. Adding to the confusion were the years of schooling we Canadians have in the French language, as well as a summer I spent in Germany learning that romance tongue. Whenever I tried to speak Spanish, my thoughts would become jumbled with all three languages, often leading to dire consequences.

Another challenging aspect of learning a foreign language is the different meaning words can have that, to the untrained ear, may sound the same. Take for instance one of our first breakfasts at Casa Blanca. The Letelliers were looked after by a wonderful young woman, Rosita, who started our days with a tastefully prepared breakfast. In inquiring what we would like for our morning meal, Karen wanted to communicate that we loved scrambled eggs, and attempted to state this fact in her Spanish. Seeing confusion in Rosita's eyes, she demonstrated what she meant by pretending to break an egg and mix the contents in a bowl. Unfortunately, the Spanish word for eggs, *huevos*, is very close to the word for a male's testicles, *huevas*. Poor Rosita must have wondered what other indignity the Canadians would bring to Chile after having men's testicles broken and stirred violently with a fork for their morning meal. As we have learned, a misplaced vowel can lead to serious problems.

Such mistakes can also lead to arguments, particularly when one is driving with one's spouse. From experience, I believe that married couples fight the most over who will provide directions to a given location, and how those directions are communicated. Without going into the male propensity not to ask for directions, we have all had a conversation that goes something like this:

"So I am to turn left at the next street," I will say.

"Right," my wife will reply.

"Turn right? I thought you said left?" I will ask, getting confused.

"Not right! I meant you are correct. Turn left, not right, all right?"

By now we will have missed the turn.

In Chile this difficulty is complicated by the fact that the Spanish word to indicate a turn to the right – *derecha* – is very close to the direction to keep going straight – *derecho*. I may just stick to taxis.

The word *huevón* is another example of how confusing Chilean Spanish can be. You hear this word everywhere you go in the country, and it is obvious it has a much different connotation when used in different contexts. The word's literal translation is "big egg", and it can be used as a term of friendship in a greeting, similar to our slang for "buddy" or "pal", but it can also be an expression of anger or disgust – someone is an idiot, a fool, a buffoon. Confusion reins supreme as the word *huevón* is close to the Spanish for egg (*huevo*) and for testicle (*hueva*), as my wife discovered. So when requesting breakfast in the morning, in addition to potentially asking for male testicles instead of eggs, you may also be calling your waiter a big fat fool.

As I learn this language, I also wonder who decides which gender a word will take? I realize that the masculine and the feminine designations don't really imply anything, but, really, why is the word for "egg" masculine and the word for "testicle" feminine? And who says the Internet is masculine? I would have thought, given the power and mystery of the world wide web, it would more appropriately be a feminine word.

On another occasion, we were in Chile for Fathers' Day. I thought that I could certainly take liberties with the language as I would be extended the courtesy of being allowed to make mistakes due to the fact that we were celebrating my position as a father of three children.

Courageously, the first person I met that morning was also a parent, and I greeted him in my best Spanish with the words "*feliz dia del papa*" – Happy Fathers' Day. I then learned that placing the right accent on the correct syllable is most important. If you accent the last syllable – paPA – you have correctly used the word for father. If you accent the first syllable – PApa – you have called someone a potato. Apparently, instead of wishing this man a happy fathers' day, I had wished him a happy day of the potato. He smiled, and shook my hand. Papa can also refer to the Pope, but I won't even think of what I might have accused His Holiness with my greeting.

We also discovered that adjectives can mean different things to different people. Take for instance the concept of hot, an important word in a country that experiences very warm summers. Looking at our phrase book, there were two words listed under the translation for hot – *calor* and *caliente*. As the latter sounded more exotic, Karen decided to use this word to describe how she felt one afternoon as we were sitting over lunch with a number of recent acquaintances. Fanning herself with a restaurant menu, she expressed that she was *muy caliente* - very hot. Unfortunately, in Chile the use of *caliente* signifies a different kind of hot, and while the men at the table smiled, their wives were not amused.

When travelling in a foreign country, I never cease to be amazed by the numerous phrase books available in airports and gift shops that are designed to help tourists get by in the new language. We have acquired a large collection of these tiny Spanish guides with the hopeless intent of improving our use of the language. However, while they can prove useful in certain situations, I am fascinated as to who chooses the phrases that are translated for you, and why they come to be chosen in the first place.

To prepare for our Chilean adventure, we purchased what is supposed to be one the best language training programs available, a series of software programs that is claimed to be used to train diplomats around the world and to provide the fastest route to becoming familiar with a new language. We were very surprised to find that among the first phrases we were taught included: "*The woman is under the table*'" and "*The children are running away*". I am still trying to think of a situation that would require the use of these phrases. Perhaps, given how much wine we drink in Chile, asking about the woman under the table is appropriate. In a similar thought, another two useful phrases translated for us in separate guidebooks were: "*I cannot climb the stairs myself*" and "*I cannot walk*". After a few pisco sours, the wonderful national drink of Chile, I know the feeling.

I found another phrase interesting – "*How much do you charge for children?*" As I already have three, I don't think I will be purchasing any more. But perhaps, if my children were the ones running away, I would have to acquire some others. Who knows? I also question when or where I would want to say "*I need boxing gloves*" or "*I would like to purchase an analog tape deck*", and I hope to God I would remember the Spanish for "*Help, I am drowning*" without having to consult the phrase book I had so stupidly left on the beach.

And in the area of personal care, we can learn how to translate the following important phrases: "*I comb my hair straight back*", "*I would like suppositories*" and "*I am flatulent*". Communicating these thoughts is seldom done at home, but I guess you never know what will come up while in a foreign country.

It can also be very illuminating to review phrase books trying to help people from other languages speak in English, one of the world's more complicated languages given its plethora of exceptions to the rules. In Chile, one enterprising man has published a guide book entitled "*Por Fin Entender a Los Gringos Es Mas Facil*", or "Finally, Listening to Gringos is Made Easy". While there are some useful sections, his attempts at phonetic spelling for many English words will have Chileans sounding like malfunctioning robots from *Lost in Space*, while I am equally perplexed at a number of the so-called popular phrases he has translated for use from Spanish into English. For example: "*If there were a cloud over my head, I would be very happy*"; "*A night has not passed in which I have not been busy personally searching his apartment*"; or "*Our purchasing manager has been widely criticized*". And in the same vein as the English to Spanish phrase books: "*I nearly died of shame when you fell down in the street yesterday.*" It is also a good thing the author informs Chileans about the different sound given to each of the vowels "B" and "V", which in Spanish can sound the same. As he correctly states, it is quite different to say that "*I am having trouble with my vowels*" than it is to say "*I am having trouble with my bowels*".

In trying to learn a new language, one is also struck by certain ironies that can be found in discovering how particular concepts and words are translated. For example, I was slightly amused to learn that the word for married – *casado* – was quite close to the Spanish for tired – *cansado*. It is also close to the word *cazado*, to hunt. A wife in a marriage is *una esposa* which is the same word, should you go to prison because you tried to sell your children to me, for a handcuff. In what had been traditionally a male-dominated society, it was no wonder that the word for pregnancy was *embarazada*. And if you were looking for some help with a spiritual problem, you might approach *el cura*, the priest, for *la cura*, the cure.

Our Spanish was seriously tested when we first met and engaged our architect and builder for the renovation of Castillo Verde. Patricio is a well-known and respected architect, and a friend of Pancho's. Although Patricio's firm and talents were typically engaged to design and construct large hotels, residential communities and embassies, he agreed to take on our project as the renovation interested him from both a design and historical perspective. We were thrilled.

Originally Karen and I had agreed that we would conduct only a minimal restoration of the Castillo. Its purchase had stretched us financially, and we thought just fixing the roof leaks, adding some interior paint and polish along with new bathroom and kitchen fixtures, would make the house livable and suit our as yet undetermined needs. Patricio, however, had different ideas.

Santiago, June 9, 2006

Dear Karen and David,

I visited Castillo Verde last week, and while this is not intended as a technical report, I wanted to give you my impressions of the property as an architect.

It definitely is a beautiful place. More than that, it gives me the impression of a house that came out of a fairy tale and has some magic in it. It looks like a place that has many stories to tell, and this gives it a lot of value. If you do get to live there, the

Castillo will always be a conversation piece for you and your guests. I really like it.

What cannot be changed is the building's structure, its stone walls, those pretty and funny-looking roofs, the location with its views, the garden, the trees, the light, the mountains, the distances, and the sensation of living in a quiet place that seems so far away from the rest of the world. It is a total composition, very complete, where nothing is in its place without a reason, where all the pieces are indispensible to obtain the whole. Let me be clear – this is the most positive and most important aspect of Castillo Verde. If all these elements were not already there, they would be impossible to obtain at any price. So all that cannot be acquired is already there, and everything that is missing or is wrong can be fixed. This is good news.

And there sure are missing and wrong things! There are two main problems.

The first has to do with planning and design. The house needs a better main garden entrance to lead to the front door, a better master bedroom, a better terrace, better windows towards the beautiful views, a better kitchen, and it needs to take more advantage of the incredible place where it is located. I already have some ideas I am sure you will like.

The second is more technical and has to do with construction, the quality of materials, finishings, engineering and technical specifications. This is more than poor, and parts are quite terrible. But all this can be fixed and replaced, and you will have a comfortable and high-spirited cottage where you can spend some wonderful times in peace and happiness. And that is a good goal.

Then comes the money subject. Depending on the price you agree to pay for the property, you could add an infinite amount to the house afterwards. However, I think you need to add an amount that is somewhere between US $50,000 and $90,000. At the lower end, you would have a poor result, and I really think it would not be worth it to spend more than the $90,000. You can cover the house with gold and it will still be the same house with the same space, location and size.

My proposal is that I prepare a preliminary design in order to ask a reliable contractor, who I will find for you, to provide an accurate estimate of the necessary investment. We can then make a final decision with all the cards in our hands.

I hope all this does not sound too crazy to you, and I look forward to hearing from you.

All the best,
Patricio

On our next trip to Chile we met with Patricio at Castillo Verde, and for the first half hour or so Patricio wandered around making notes and gazing at the exterior of the house with a practiced eye. He then began to draw furiously. When he was done, he sat us down and explained his vision for the Castillo, which included an entire new front entrance hall extending up the full height of the house, lifting, replacing and adding a new roof, a new room and entrance at the side, new balconies off each bedroom over the river, as well as a number of other major initiatives. The wiring and plumbing would have to be replaced, new stonework added, new windows and doors, new slate floors, and a host of other improvements.

I wondered what part of our concept of an inexpensive and modest renovation he had not understood. It must be the language again.

However, the more we looked at the concepts he had drawn, and the more we understood his vision for Castillo Verde, the more we were attracted to the idea depending, of course, on the cost. We asked him to take the next step to have proper drawings prepared and have a builder quote on the project.

On our following trip, we met at Patricio's office to be introduced to Rodrigo, the recommended builder for the renovation. Rodrigo had done a number of projects for Patricio, including Patricio's own house. During our introductions, the nuance of language again raised its ugly head as, when Rodrigo asked if we spoke Spanish, Karen replied "*un pico*". Unfortunately, she had replied to his question by calling him a small penis. Following nervous laughter and extensive apologies, we moved on.

We discussed budgets and timing, and, after a lengthy review of the drawings and options available to us, we agreed to move ahead with the much larger project based on meeting the proposed budgets and time frame. The meeting occurred in August 2006, and we were assured we would have at least a bedroom and bathroom ready for us by Christmas that year. The total cost of the project was estimated at approximately 43 million pesos, or about US $85,000.

Little did we know that it would take almost a year longer and cost almost three times as much to obtain that bedroom and bathroom, and to complete the project.

CHAPTER TWELVE

THE CARABINEROS ARE OUR FRIENDS

As our bi-monthly trips to Chile began to increase in frequency, our friends realized that this Chilean adventure was a reality for us. I think they all thought it had been a typical "fall in love with a holiday destination" situation, but that we would succumb to a healthy dose of sobriety upon a return to the real world.

We have all done this. We visit a fabulous island in the Caribbean, a character-filled, sun-drenched, colorful beach resort in the Mediterranean, or the chateau laden wine regions of Tuscany or Provence, and we see ourselves living there. We might visit a real estate agent or cruise sites on the Internet, but soon, on returning home, the realities of jobs, careers, children and just making ends meet, drives the dream away.

Another reason we might put the vision of living in a foreign country on the back burner is the cultural difference between where we are comfortable, and what might await us if we were to adopt a different lifestyle far from home.

This was certainly one of our concerns, and for many of our friends who were worried about safety and security. Is not South America filled with armed guerillas kidnapping and holding for ransom supposedly wealthy gringos? Are not pickpockets everywhere, murder rampant, crime pervasive, and corruption and bribes the mainstay of these crumbling third-world economies? Are we nuts to be giving up the comforts of home for the unknown of a relatively misunderstood country where, just a few short years ago, ordinary citizens were being dragged from their homes by a fascist regime, never to be seen again?

Certainly we were ever watchful of signs that these perceptions were a reality, but we have been pleasantly surprised by the calm, order and general respect for a civilized rule of law we have experienced in Chile. One of the reasons this sense of civil order persists in the country, I believe, is the existence of the Chilean national police force, once an arm of brutal repression, but today a modern police force that appears to command respect for their services.

The national uniformed police force is called the *Carabineros de Chile*. The *Carabineros* were officially formed in 1927 when the separate police forces of Santiago, Valparaiso and the *Policia Rural* were combined under one roof. Their stated mission is to maintain or re-establish order and security in Chilean society, provide service to the community and, in a war, act like a paramilitary force. All members of the *Carabineros* have undergone military training. And while they are an independent force separate to the military, they are ultimately under the direction of the *Ministerio de Defensa Nacional* (Minister of Defence) and can be integrated into the armed forces during a state of emergency, as they were under General Pinochet's regime.

Unlike many Latin American police forces, honesty and integrity are extremely important to the *Carabineros de Chile*. Any form of bribery is liable to serious punishment, both for the civilian and for the policeman, and many travelers, familiar with bribing their way out of a traffic ticket in other South and Central American countries, have found themselves temporarily imprisoned for trying the same tactic in Chile.

The *Carabineros*, who wear dark green uniforms and ride around in small cars, armed vehicles with water canons, and very cool off-road motorcycles, are a fit, strong and no-nonsense group of young men and women. Referred to commonly as "*pacos*", they are respected, if not a bit feared, by the citizens of Chile. These are not the guys we see at home eating their donuts and waiting in cruisers to fill their quota of speeding tickets.

A case in point was the recent murder of a young *Carabinero* during an attempted bank robbery. For days the newspapers, radio and television were filled with details of the manhunt for the killers, as well as sympathetic coverage of the young officer's family. His funeral was broadcast on national television with Chile's President attending. In a city of almost seven million people, I was struck by the attention and sympathy extended to the death of one police officer. In large North American cities the death of a police officer seems to have become almost a daily event not attracting nearly the same amount of attention or respect.

I have mixed feelings as I see the *pacos* around the country. Clearly they are doing a good job as crime rates are quite low. The restaurant below Castillo Verde was recently held up by armed thugs, and all were quickly rounded up, arrested by the *Carabineros,* and the stolen property returned. Yet this is the same police force that was an active and brutal arm of the Pinochet regime, and I wonder how many of their officers have a much darker past.

So far we have had two interesting encounters with the *Carabineros de Chile.*

The first occurred on one of Santiago's busiest thoroughfares, *Avenida Amerigo Vespuchio.* This six and eight lane highway runs through the centre of city from north to south, and comprises one link in the connected roadway system designed to move traffic efficiently within and through the city, and to provide a speedy exit to neighboring residential areas. Suffice to say it is a very busy and very important road.

We were driving along *Vespuchio* one evening, as were thousands of other vehicles taking dads and moms home from work, conveying goods to strengthen the Chilean economy, delivering important documents, and many others on important tasks. Suddenly, in my rear view mirror, I saw a cavalcade of *carabineros* on high powered motorcycles approaching rapidly, flashing their lights, sounding their sirens and waving everyone over to stop at the side of the road. Clearly this must be an emergency of some sort, or perhaps an important politician being safely guided out of harms way. Curious, we waited to see what would appear. And then it came, a bus carrying a soccer team returning to their home field and locker room after finishing an away match. I guess soccer really is important in Chile.

Our second encounter with the *Caribineros de Chile* took place as we were driving back to Pirque from the coast after visiting *Isla Negra,* Pablo Neruda's seaside home. We were on a four-lane highway, modern and well-maintained. You have to be very vigilant driving in Chile as you can be moving quickly down the six-lane Pan-American, the major north-south route that travels the length of the country, when suddenly a family will be strolling across the highway to catch a bus on the other side. Chileans seem to treat all roads, no matter how busy, as their own. They do not distinguish between meandering along a dirt back road on their bicycle or on foot, and doing the same thing on a major high-speed highway. It can be quite disconcerting.

With this trait well in mind, I noticed a figure walking slowly across our highway from left to right. I realized that if I were to maintain my present speed and highway lane, and this person did not wait on the median or start to run, we would certainly reach a collision point very soon. There was no one else or any other vehicle on the highway in either direction – it was just this person and my car. As I continued to watch their progress, and determined they were not going to change direction or speed, I pulled out into the left-hand passing lane of our empty divided highway to make certain the pedestrian had time to cross safely and unimpeded. But as I approached the figure, the familiar green uniform of the *Carabineros* came into view, and the Officer pointed at me to pull over.

As I waited for him to approach, I pulled out the car rental agreement, my passport and Canadian driver's license, and rolled down the window. He leaned in to the car, wished me a good day, and then said something I did not understand. I explained that we were *turistas* from Canada, spoke little Spanish, and handed him all the papers and documents. He examined each carefully, and then stated that we were *touristas*. We agreed.

He asked me to step out of the car, and began to speak to me slowly, deliberately, and at great length. I had no idea what he was saying and, from past experience, knew I should not simply nod my head as though I understood. I continued to look quizzically at him, shrugging my shoulders with a polite smile on my face. However, it became clear that this Officer was not going to let us go until I understood what I had done wrong. I started to pay more attention, and through extensive sign language, drawing pictures in the dirt, gesticulating and moving in and out of the roadway, I suddenly had an epiphany and understanding of what I had done wrong.

I had driven in the passing lane when I did not need to pass anything.

I initially thought I should try and explain that I had pulled into the passing lane to avoid either hitting the Officer, or forcing him to run across the road, but quickly realized this might keep us with him for another hour or two. My motivation to contravene this serious infraction of the Chilean Highway Traffic Act had been with the best of intentions, but I deemed there was no way that I would win this argument, nor would I be able to properly explain the reasons with my rudimentary Spanish. I took the easy way, nodding my understanding by using my hands as cars to demonstrate when it was, and was not, acceptable to use the passing lane. The Officer smiled, a bit sternly I thought, realizing I was now familiar with this particular law. He shook my hand, and bade us a safe trip.

As we pulled away, I had an increased respect for the *Carabineros de Chile*. This man could have simply ticketed us or sent us on our way realizing we were simple, stupid tourists who did not speak the language. But first and foremost he was an officer of the law, and he wanted to make sure we did not make the same mistake again. Rest assured that even on the busiest highways, I now pull back out of the passing lane whenever I use it, and, if there is little traffic, I never drift to the left.

The Officer also had a really big gun.

This sense of law, order, and the right way of doing things did not, unfortunately, seem to extend to our construction crew at Castillo Verde.

CHAPTER THIRTEEN

THE PROJECT BEGINS

The renovation, reconstruction and renaissance of Castillo Verde commenced at the beginning of October 2006, with an approved budget of approximately 43 million pesos, or roughly US $85,000. Rodrigo would manage the project, using Patricio's designs that had now been converted into proper drawings and written specifications. Rodrigo explained that he would put one of his top men, Juan, on site to ensure everything went well, and that Juan would hire all the workmen. In Chile, workmen in almost any profession or activity are referred to as *maestros*, a connotation in English that we frequently questioned as we moved through the project.

The initial labour involved some significant demolition of both internal and external walls. The internal work contemplated removing a thick concrete wall between the dining room and the kitchen, and another to extend the dining room into a large adjacent downstairs bathroom that we were replacing in another location. The wide cypress plank floors throughout the downstairs, except the living room, were being removed, with the planks being saved to replace damaged pieces upstairs, and to be used in the new rooms we were adding to the Castillo.

The removal of the walls was our first clue that things were done differently here. Instead of utilizing large powerful electric or pneumatic machines to break up the concrete walls, which in places were almost twelve inches thick, we found an army of men with sledge hammers, pick axes, shovels and rakes pounding away for several days. It was intense, difficult and strenuous manual labour, with pieces of wall flying around and clouds of dust engulfing a workforce that had never heard of protective eyewear, helmets or safety shoes. With her background in construction, Karen was horrified and insisted this safety equipment be provided for all of the *maestros*. I am not sure much of it was used when we were not present on site, as on a number of visits we found hard hats conveniently being used to hold nails, screws and other loose fastening systems, as well as coolers for drinks.

As the floors were raised we discovered that the house, although solidly built and properly engineered to withstand the strongest earthquakes, had no real foundations. Pulling up the floorboards, to our surprise we found nothing underneath but dirt, rocks and boulders and little else. We had arranged for two engineering studies to be done on the property prior to completing the purchase, and a third, older report had been provided to us by Carlos during our negotiations to buy Castillo Verde. All attested to the soundness of the property and its structural integrity. In addition, the house had survived a very powerful earthquake in 1985, one that had leveled many homes and buildings in the vicinity and caused significant destruction. Still, seeing the bare earth and rock under the floors did cause us a moment or two of concern.

In addition to the earthquake worry, the lack of foundations under the house led to the first obstacle in the project, and naturally the first upward adjustment to the project's budget. New concrete would have to be poured to support the floors, but before pouring the raw dirt surface would have to be cleared and all of the large boulders protruding from the ground removed. We had chosen some beautiful dark granite tiles for the kitchen and dining room, and they required a level, smooth surface for proper installation.

Out came the sledge hammers, pick axes, shovels and rakes again, although they did have to resort to some heavy duty cutting equipment to assist in the removal of some particularly large boulders. Gravel was brought in, tamped down, at which time rough, then fine concrete was poured on top and leveled. All of this was done by hand with wheel barrows, buckets and shovels. It took forever.

Outside was an even more daunting task. We had agreed to build an entire new entrance to the Castillo facing the garden, which involved removing most of the exterior stone wall on that side of the house, as well as the entire leaking and rotting roof. Foundations had to be dug and prepared for the new entrance, and then forms and supports built to hold the rebar and concrete that would comprise the new walls that rose approximately thirty feet from ground level. These walls would then be clad in granite facing that resembled the stone blocks making up the rest of the house.

On one of our inspections the concrete pour for the new walls was well underway. One man stood on top of a scaffold with a rope. He quickly donned his hard hat when he saw us. The rope was attached to a small bucket. Out in the driveway a small rotary concrete mixer was in operation, the kind you might rent at your local hardware store to pour a few post holes. Two men filled the mixer's receptacle with the correct proportions of sand, aggregate and cement, added the water, at which time another maestro turned the machine on, and then tipped it to fill a wheelbarrow with the mixture. The full wheelbarrow was trundled over to the wall where another man shoveled some of the concrete mix into the bucket, which was then hoisted up and poured into the formwork.

The new entrance hall called for three very large, very high and very thick walls to be poured. I am not sure how many yards of concrete were required, but it was a lot, easily two or three truck loads had North American procedures been followed. And all of this was being accomplished one bucket at a time. I thought of suggesting that two buckets and two wheelbarrows might be used, but then my construction experience was limited and who was I to say that we did not do things like this in Canada.

The interior and exterior demolition, and the wall construction, seemed to take forever. We would go back to Canada and return three weeks later, only to find the same *maestros* with the same bucket and the same system. It drove us crazy, particularly as we were on a cost-plus contract and knew the longer it took, the more we would pay.

Not that the *maestros* did not work long and hard hours. They arrived early, with quite a few bunking down overnight on the floor of the adobe house rather than travel the many miles to wherever they lived. They worked until the sun went down, often seven or eight at night. They did, however, avail themselves of long lunches and a bit of a siesta in the afternoon. A few times on hot days we found them splashing around in the small swimming pool located beside the turret. A study of workplace efficiency performed by The Economist magazine implied that, of all South American countries, Chileans worked the hardest, but were the least productive. We were hopeful our project would prove this trait to be false.

Meantime, the roof was being removed and new supports and beams installed. Before this work could progress to any great extent, we had to decide if we were going to add the new laundry room off the kitchen. This, of course, was another addition to the contract and required a further upward revision in the price. Nevertheless we agreed to proceed as not only would we need the space for our laundry and storage, the structure nicely balanced the proportions of the house and its new roof lines.

On a construction job in Chile, when the last piece of roof support is installed, it is customary to hold a party for your *maestros*. This celebration, called a *tijerale,* is an important milestone and recognition that we valued the work being done by our *maestros*. A Chilean flag, and in our case, accompanied by a Canadian flag, is flown from the new roof to indicate the completion of this stage of the project, and a sign that the *tijerale* will be held. The problem for us was that we were not in the country when this happened, and there was a bit of concern on the part of the *maestros* as to whether we would return for the required revelry. Apparently it is also very bad luck not to hold this celebration.

The first *tijerale* we attended was at a new cabin Pancho and Angela were building in the lovely little seaside fishing village of Maitencillo. They had purchased some land high up on a hill overlooking the beach and ocean, and were constructing a vacation property for their family that had been designed to resemble a ship's prow jutting out from the cliff. They had finished their roof, and we were invited to attend the celebrations. Not only did we raise a glass to the new home, but this was also the day that General Pinochet died.

On a number of our trips I brought gifts for various people that, in my opinion, were distinctly Canadian. I had given Juan, the head *maestro* at Castillo Verde, a Toronto Maple Leafs hockey cap. For the rest of our *maestros*, I provided Canadian flag lapel pins – one *maestro* asked for two pins so that he could use them as earrings. At Pancho's *tijerale* I presented the head *maestro* with a hat from our local football team, the Hamilton Tiger Cats. The man thanked me, but as we translated the name of the team, the other *maestros* started to laugh and make fun of him. Apparently, they teased that, with his wife, he may think he was a tiger, but really he was a little kitten. With a frown he immediately removed the hat and I did not see it again. Clearly, this was yet another example of how language and culture often did not move easily between our two countries.

Once we learned that the auspicious milestone of finishing the roof had been achieved at Castillo Verde, we hastily returned to Chile from Canada to organize our own *tijerale*. We engaged a nearby traditional Chilean restaurant, *La Vaquita Echa*, to cater the event, and they arrived on the appointed day with tables and chairs, large barbecues, as well as empanadas, beef, chicken and salads for the meal. I obtained a few cases of wine from a nearby winery, as well as cans of local beer and a lot of the soft drink Coca Cola – Chileans love their Coke.

It was a wonderful celebration. We all sat under our glorious fig tree which provided shade and cool from the hot sun. The *asado* was perfectly prepared with lots to eat and drink for everyone. Including our neighbours the Leteliers, Pancho and Angela, as well as other new friends from Santiago, we totaled about forty people.

A highlight of the day was the arrival of Santo Rubio, a local musician and story-teller from a very old family who lived in nearby La Puntilla. Santo had brought his *guitarron*, a traditional Chilean twenty-five stringed guitar-like instrument that he played to accompany his songs. Santo is much more than a local musician. He was blind from birth, and in Chile one of the tasks for the sightless is to pray for you in Churches and at specific shrines. Santo was such a person, and was revered by the people who lived in and around the area. He was also the repository of much of the oral legend and stories from the region, and most of his songs told these tales. He also sang many popular ballads, to which everyone joined in and sang along. During the party he even composed a song about the two Canadians who came to Chile to live in a beautiful Castillo on the hill. We were touched.

As the afternoon turned into a beautiful, warm evening, we left the *maestros* to finish the wine and beer and enjoy their time with Santo, singing along with him on all their favorite songs. Not surprisingly, there was little accomplished the next day, but we were thanked profusely by everyone involved and told it was one of the better *tijerales* the *maestros* had attended. Their thanks were given with big grins on everyone's face, no doubt remembering my speech of thanks delivered the prior evening in my pidgin Spanish during which I am sure I misused words, or worse, as was our custom in Chile, referred to something horribly obscene rather than complimentary.

Over the next few months work progressed at Castillo Verde. Once the outside walls and roof were completed, everyone moved inside to perform the finishing work. As inspections were carried out, we were told that there was some concern over the state of the water pipes and electrical wiring in the house. We had thought we could utilize the existing services as all were buried within the concrete walls and seemed to work. However, Rodrigo told us that he could not warrant the water and electrical system unless new pipes, conduit and wire were installed. He was also quite concerned that what existed was old, damaged and not dependable. We agreed to install new systems, recognizing that this would involve using the same manual labour and hand tools to hack and claw channels into all the interior walls of the house in order to run new pipes and conduit. Naturally, yet another upward revision to the budget was required, but at least we knew we would have dependable water and electricity.

At the same time we decided to install a hot water heating system in the house. If we were digging holes and trenches into the walls, we might as well install the pipes to access radiators in all the rooms. Installing central heat is quite unusual in Chile. The winters are not too cold, and if the temperatures do fall below a comfort level, people use fireplaces or temporary space heaters to generate temporary warmth. In addition, natural gas, propane and electricity is very expensive by North American standards. Yet installing pipes and radiators at Castillo Verde would ensure we would be comfortable no matter how cold it got outside, and the addition would certainly enhance the value and prestige of the property. We agreed, realizing yet another budget revision was in order.

To Rodrigo's credit, he did keep us apprised of the mounting costs of the project, and provided detailed summaries of materials and time spent as we progressed. What had started out as a 43 million peso estimate had climbed to approximately 85 million pesos by now, almost double our original budget. Having done a renovation at home in Canada, and talking to friends about what such a project would cost there, despite the increase in cost we knew we were getting a lot done for much less than it would cost at home.

Still, we were not sure we were getting the best price for materials, or that we were not being charged more than the going rate for labour given that we were perceived as rich gringos from Canada. John, a lifelong friend from Canada who was the first to visit our project from home, had recently built a new cottage in Ontario's lake district, and commented our work would easily cost two or three times as much in Canada. At the same time, he looked at me as though he thought we were insane to have tackled such a massive renovation in a foreign country ten hours away by airplane and in a language we did not speak. He was probably right.

At one point, toward the end of the project, we had the following people busy at Castillo Verde: fifteen maestros working for Rodrigo; Arnaldo, an electrician installing new wires; Aladino, a plumber replacing pumps and pipes for the water delivery; Hernan working on our kitchen cabinets and book cases; Julio, working in the garden while the adobe house was being repaired; Nino building stone walls and paths on the hillside; Humberto welding protective iron grates for the windows; and Veloso helping as best he could. It was a bit chaotic, but things were getting done.

And we persevered, maintaining a tight eye on the project. We also began a process whereby one of us would fly to Chile, unannounced, at least every other week to inspect the work and assess progress. These surprise visits kept the *maestros* on their toes, and ensured the pace of work was maintained. These inspections were also very illuminating, as on one visit we noticed that the *maestros* had completed one wall of the new entrance hall but forgot to add an important window. It was in the drawings and specifications, they had simply not bothered to refer to them.

As the project started to come together, we realized that we did, in fact, have true *maestros* working for us in every sense of the word. Although the pace was maddening slow, the quality of the work was superlative, and everyone took great pride in their craft and their assigned tasks. They were also quick to remedy mistakes, and, for the most part listened patiently to us as we tried to express ourselves in halting Spanish.

Of all the *maestros* working on the site, none was as conscientious and diligent as Humberto, and as time progressed he became a very important part of our lives in Chile.

CHAPTER FOURTEEN

THE SECOND SPANISH INVASION

hilean society, to our North American sensibilities, appears very stratified with a wealthy and influential upper class, a well-off middle class, and a massive number of people who, to our standards, live in abject poverty with little opportunity to better themselves. As the country has prospered over the last decade, quality education has become a key objective for the government, and significant progress has been made. More children are being schooled, and more are able to attend post-secondary education at the numerous public and private universities and colleges located throughout the country. Despite these improvements, a distinct and long-standing class system prevails, and many are frustrated with the inability to improve their lot in life.

During one trip, we experienced a student strike. In an effort to accelerate improved and more universally available education, all of the students in the country staged a series of demonstrations, forcing the closure of their schools as they took their desks and chairs out into the streets to protest the slow pace of change. Despite the strength of the economy, and the government's promise to divert much of this wealth to education, many students were still without books or school supplies. It was quite something to see thousands of uniformed kids peacefully manning barricades and blocking streets while designated spokespersons, some as young as 14 years old, faced the police and the media to present their grievances.

When we first purchased Castillo Verde, Luis Veloso was living in the property's adobe house. He was somewhere between 80 and 90 years old – we never did ascertain his true age – and although a hard and diligent worker, we were concerned the duties we needed in the future would far exceed his abilities and his energy. He had worked for the previous owner Carlos for many years, each day walking about four miles to Carlos' new home up the mountainside to perform heavy manual labour in his almond orchards. At the end of each day, he would return to Castillo Verde to keep an eye on things, living mostly outside sleeping in a hammock and cooking over an open fire. He also, apparently, enjoyed a drink or two in the evening.

Over time we learned that he had family living in nearby towns, and in fact also had a wife who lived elsewhere. Apparently many *huasos* prefer to live apart from their spouse, earning money and sending it home for mother to raise the children. We surmised Veloso had become accustomed to this lifestyle and wanted to maintain it as long as possible.

As the project progressed, we got to know Humberto very well. He had worked for Pancho as a welder on a number of his public art installations and sculptures, and also did general contracting work such as plumbing, electrical and a number of other trades. We learned that he was a Pentecostal Christian, he was married to Maria, and that they had two small children - Samuel who was eight and Elyou who was three. Karen and I both agreed he would be the perfect person to look after our old but hopefully rejuvenated house and property, as he could do most of the maintenance and upkeep we would need while providing a higher level of security than the much, much older Veloso.

As an example of Humberto's valuable contribution to our new lives, we had arranged to have a telephone line and Internet service installed at the house so that, when we moved in, we would be able to communicate more easily and inexpensively. The communications supplier to San Juan de Pirque was Telefonica, a Spanish company with a large presence in Chile.

When we first contacted them, Telefonica advised us that they did not provide telephones and Internet service to foreigners. When I convinced them that, although we were not Chilean citizens, we did in fact own a property in the country, they agreed to take the process further. This step took three separate visits to their offices, many telephone calls, and the provision of a number of official papers and documents that I had to have notarized. Chileans love to have documents notarized, and notary offices are everywhere, even in the smallest of towns.

Once Telefonica agreed that we could be provided with their services, they then informed us that they did not, in fact, offer these services in the vicinity of our house. This was surprising as both the Letelier property next door, as well as other neighbours around us, were all using Telefonica. After searching databases for an extended period of time, they admitted this was the case, and processed our application. However, to get connected, we would have to contact the installation people at another location to arrange for a date when they could come.

As you can imagine by now, we had to go to another office, stand in line, and start all over again, providing passports, statements, notarized documents, explaining our situation, insisting that, yes, they did actually service our neighbourhood, and that we were a decent credit risk for the $40 a month we would be spending. They finally agreed to install the services within the ensuing two weeks.

Almost three weeks later, a tiny Telefonica truck appeared at Castillo Verde with one man and a clipboard. He was there to assess the situation, he explained, and ensure the installation crew brought all the necessary equipment and supplies. He looked around, made some notes, and left. We heard nothing for another two weeks and, after numerous telephone calls, surprisingly the same man re-appeared, in the same truck, to install the wires and hook us up. When he left, we finally had Internet and a telephone.

The telephone was quite mysterious. We could not dial any long distance numbers, nor could we dial a cell phone, even one registered in Chile. Toll-Free numbers could also not be accessed. We then learned that all of these functions were separate services at additional cost. In fact, the only numbers we could dial were our immediate neighbours. We decided to maintain this minimal level of service as we had a fully functional Chilean cell phone, and the service was quite good at a reasonable cost. The telephone line was only necessary for the Internet connection.

The Internet was quite good, a high speed service that seemed to meet all of our needs, except for one issue – quite often the service would cut off at around 8.00 pm in the evening, reconnecting again in the middle of the night. Some evenings it would stay connected, others it would disappear at different times. We called Telefonica, and after a number of conversations and initial denials that it could be happening, we were offered the explanation that, once the sun went down, it became much colder, causing our wires to stretch and temporarily sever the connection, During the night, the wires recovered, and we were back in business. Apparently the laws of physics were different in Chile as they related to the reaction of copper to temperature changes.

I mentioned this rational to Humberto who, tracing the wire installed by Telefonica from the house to the utility pole on the street, noticed that it had been strung through the branches of a number of trees, He re-strung the wire to avoid these branches, and we have had steady Internet service ever since. As Michael, one of our new neighbours, stated: "Telefonica is the second very unwelcome invasion of Chile by the Spanish".

On one of our next visits we invited Humberto to bring his family to the Castillo on a Sunday, the *maestros'* day off. We prepared a nice lunch, including soft drinks and sweets for the children. The family arrived punctually at the invited time – not an easy task when you are at the mercy of the rural "yellow death" bus system – and we had a thoroughly enjoyable afternoon. The children were polite and well behaved, and clearly both kids were intelligent and curious. We liked them immediately. Maria was very outgoing and talked with us, an unusual trait in Chile as wives for the most part are quite shy and normally defer to their husbands. This was not the case in Humberto's family, and Maria questioned us about our lives in Canada, our children, and told us a great deal about where and how they lived. They were obviously a very happy family.

As the afternoon progressed and we became more familiar and comfortable with each other, we asked Humberto and Maria if they would consider coming to live at Castillo Verde and look after us. We wanted a younger family to be on the property as the husband could do the outside work while the wife could take care of us and the house when we were there. We knew Humberto was up to the task, and then some, but could Maria cook and clean for us? She explained she had done this before, and that, if we did not mind traditional Chilean food, she would be happy to cook for us. Besides, she said, her empanadas were exquisite.

The empanada, the most prevalent of traditional Chilean dishes, is the hot dog or hamburger of Chile. They are available everywhere – sold from roadside stands, or from people's homes who display a white flag, in all restaurants, in cemeteries when visiting the departed, at sporting events, rodeos, fairs, circuses, anywhere people gather you will find someone selling empanadas. Everyone has their favorite style and ingredients, and everyone has a strongly held opinion about what should make up this Chilean staple. In essence, an empanada is a tortilla filled with seasoned meat, egg and olives, or as an alternative with seafood or with cheese. There are a few other variations, but these are the three main versions. The empanada is eaten by hand with *pebre,* a hot chile-based salsa. They can be small or quite large, are traditionally baked in an outdoor wood-fired oven, and they are delicious.

The second most popular traditional Chilean menu item is *pastel de choclo,* and recipe variations for this staple are widespread. Similar to the English shepherd's pie, it combines chicken, corn, beef, vegetables and olives in a casserole covered in mashed potatoes and cheese and baked in an oven. *Pastel de choclo* can also be found in most restaurants and at road-side stands everywhere in the country.

The roadside drink-of-choice is *mote con huesillo,* a cold sweet juice made from stewed peaches. The juice is accompanied by a peeled stewed peach as well as an inch or two of wheat germ. It is an incredible cure for a hangover, and if I were smart I would bring this functional restorative to North America packaged for grocery store aisles.

Lunches normally start with a *cazuela,* a clear broth containing rice, potato, some vegetables, a corn cob, a large piece of squash, and a quarter chicken. A variation to this is *marisco,* a sort of bouillabaisse using a seafood broth and filled with various shellfish, rice, vegetables and often a chorizo sausage.

Chilean seafood is very popular and very accessible, and includes salmon, *corvina* (seabass), *congrio* (a long, narrow salt-water fish resembling an eel), *locos* (abalone), *manchas* (razor clams), *almejas* (clams), *canrejo* (crab), *erizos* (sea urchin), *pulpo* or *calamari* (octopus), and *ostiones* (scallops). Fish is prepared *al vapor* (steamed), or *a la plancha* (grilled). *Ceviche* is also a delicacy, raw fish or shellfish marinated in lemon juice overnight and served cold.

Being close to the pampas of Argentina, all things beef are also found in *parillas*, restaurants that primarily serve grilled beef cuts, as well as chicken, lamb and sausage. A popular traditional meal in a *parilla* is *lomo a la pobre*, or poor man's steak. It consists of a seared steak and French fried potatoes covered with two fried eggs. Chile also has its own version of kobe beef, called *wagyu*, although it is very expensive and saved for special occasions.

Chilean deserts, or *postre*, are designed for those with a real sweet-tooth. Fresh fruits are always available, but traditional *postre* will always include a very sugary cake with loads of icing, and anything filled or covered with *dulce de leche*, a very sweet, rich and thick caramel sauce. One of my favorites is *cuchufli*, a long, cigar-shaped chocolate covered biscuit filled with *dulce de leche*. Your teeth may ache after eating one, but it is well-deserved pain.

The one aspect of Chilean dining I imagine I will never get accustomed to is their obsession with instant coffee. With the world having been conquered by designer coffees, lattes, espressos and many other varieties and combinations, and fine coffee growing countries such as Brazil nearby, it is strange to sit down to a meal and be offered, at the end, a cup of hot water with a little pouch of Nescafe nestled beside it, normally sweetened with an artificial sugar. This custom is everywhere, and unless you are fortunate enough to be dining in one of Santiago's or Valparaiso's fine restaurants who are able to brew real coffee for you on request, the instant variety may be the only choice you have.

After discussing compensation and timing with Maria and Humberto, we shook hands, then hugged, and the deal was consummated. As they stood to leave, Maria had tears in her eyes. She explained that they had never thought they would get a chance to better themselves, or offer their children the opportunity to escape the poverty they had known. Now, they would be moving from a small, 200 square foot apartment in a squalid government-subsidized tenement building located in a very rough neighborhood, to a much larger 1,200 square foot house in a more healthy and pleasant rural setting. Humberto and Maria would have their own bedroom, a living room in which to relax with their family and friends, as well as a separate kitchen and bathroom. The children would also have their own bedroom, as well as a large and secure courtyard in which to play. Most importantly, they would have access to much better schools in and around Pirque. They were very grateful, and we were very happy, both to be helping them and providing ourselves with the comfort of knowing both Castillo Verde and its guests would be well looked after.

We agreed that Humberto and his family would begin their move into Castillo Verde in the new year, with Humberto installing himself initially to continue his work on the Castillo as well as to prepare the adobe house for the arrival of his family three months hence. To thank Veloso for his years of service to the Castillo, and for taking such good care of the property during the difficult renovation period, we presented him with a significant gift of cash and allowed him to take all the new furniture we had purchased for him. He was very thankful and, in a final irony, his son-in-law who turned up to help move him arrived in a Telefonica truck. Why Veloso had not asked him to assist with our telephone and Internet problems is a mystery that will now never be solved.

One thing that Veloso and Humberto most likely had not encountered in their lives, at least so far, was the bureaucracy that accompanied obtaining a mortgage in Chile. When we agreed to purchase Castillo Verde, we decided to finance part of the purchase price with a Chilean loan. One of our largest Canadian financial institutions had a major presence throughout South America, and with interest rates much lower in Chile than in Canada, and the opportunity to lay off some of the risk of owning a property in a foreign country on a local bank, we arranged a meeting in one of their main branches in Santiago.

In Chile, banks will provide a mortgage for up to 90% of the value of a property. However, the mortgage is not based on what you pay for a house, but what the bank appraises its value to be, and the two amounts can be quite different. For example, the appraisal done by the bank valued Castillo Verde at just under two-thirds of what we had agreed to pay for the property. Apparently this wide discrepancy in valuations is quite normal in Chile, and has something to do with the illiquid nature of the residential property market that had existed in recent years, and the fact that most Chileans acquire properties without bank loans. Thus there is little comprehensive market information about real estate prices, and each mortgage is based on an evaluation from an independent firm. How they base their assessment remains a mystery, but we nevertheless decided to move ahead.

As we were hoping to obtain a higher valuation on which to calculate our mortgage, we agreed with our bank representative that we would not formally apply for the loan until after Carlos had completed all of the so-called improvements and upgrades he needed to make in order for the municipality to approve his transferring ownership to us. We believed once these projects had been completed, we would obtain a higher valuation. Fortunately, we were correct and we were able to obtain an approved mortgage for the amount we wanted, at a very reasonable interest rate. The interest rate would float on a monthly basis, but was also capped at a maximum. In a country that had seen rapid and significant inflation in the past, this was a very comforting arrangement.

There were, however, a couple of complicating, and illuminating, aspects to the mortgage. The first was its restatement into the ever-present UF monetary system. Not only was the principle amount stated in UF, so too were the blended monthly mortgage payments. As a result, not only did we have to convert the UF amount each month into pesos, we had the added risk of the exchange rate between Canada and Chile. These issues created mathematical machinations that were far beyond my meager mind, and I simply determined to trust everyone at the bank and let our exposure ride with the winds of international trade balances, copper prices, inflation forecasts, currency movements and everything else that might affect our loan.

The second interesting aspect of the mortgage was my discovery, as we signed reams of documents and declarations, that everything was in my wife's name – the ownership of Castillo Verde, the mortgage, our chequeing account at the bank, our vehicle, everything. I was referred to simply as *el otro*, or the "other", on all official documents and statements. Now I was not sure if I should be comforted or alarmed at this development. Certainly Karen had begun the process with the lawyer and the bank, and we both took some measure of delight in having a woman secure the title and the loans in a country that still viewed the male half of a marriage as somewhat more equal.

Yet I thought at least they could record my name somewhere. What if there were another *otro* I did not know about? What if they did not know who the *otro* was? Could I use the appellation as a title or a name? Would this new alias allow me to sign cheques and conduct banking business as *el orto*? Perhaps I could don dark glasses, grow a pencil-thin mustache, sport black clothing and wear a cape? Would a sword be out of character? I have always wanted to brandish a sword. Maybe a t-shirt with an appropriate logo could be designed, and I could ride through the mountains robbing the rich and... You get my point.

The truth was that the banking system in Chile was not really set up to accommodate joint accounts. Everything had to be in one person's name, and that person, in our case, was Karen. When we first started banking, they set up two accounts, one in my name, and one in Karen's. When we wired money from Canada, it often went into a different account than anticipated, causing all sorts of chaos when mortgage payments were withdrawn from accounts with insufficient funds, while the other account had lots of cash sitting dormant. After a series of meetings, we closed my account and moved to what we thought was a joint account. Despite allowing both signatures, it remained in Karen's name, and I was designated as *el otro*. Apparently I am destined to be *el otro* for all of our Chile transactions, and I have now become quite comfortable and accustomed to the situation. The t-shirt and sword, however, remain a wonderful fantasy.

CHAPTER FIFTEEN
IN VINO VERITAS

One of the consolations of a dubious supply of safe drinking water in rural Chile is the opportunity to sample the country's fine selection of domestically produced wines. As oenophiles around the world have discovered, Chile has grown to become one of the leading exporters of wine with extensive and mature vineyards producing some of the world's highest quality, award-winning red and white vintages.

The first grapes destined for making wine arrived in Chile with the Spanish conquistadores in the mid-16th century. Catholic missionaries who had accompanied the soldiers demanded the sacramental wines necessary to celebrate their religious rites, while the soldiers looked forward to satisfying their thirst following hot days travelling and fighting the Indians. The initial plantings came from cuttings made in Peru of vines originally transported from Spain. Called *pais*, this grape became the most widely available in Chile and the raw material for much of its early wine making.

Despite its close ties to Spain, Chilean winemaking has been most influenced by French techniques, particularly from the Bordeaux region. With many Chileans becoming extremely wealthy during the late eighteenth and early nineteenth centuries from the country's burgeoning mining industry, more sophisticated tastes were turning to European wines, and numerous large and elaborate haciendas were built in the countryside surrounded by vineyards. A Chilean winemaker named Silvestre Ochagavia is credited with bringing the first French vines to the Maipo River Valley, including Cabernet Sauvignon, Merlot, Pinot Noir, Sauvignon Blanc, Semillon and Riesling. In 1870 Don Maximo Errazuriz hired a French oenologist to oversee the planting of his vineyard and wine production, and his business became the first Chilean winery dedicated to international varietals. Soon, the *pais* grape was relegated to the cheaper, bulk-produced more rustic wines destined for local consumption.

The true renaissance of Chilean winemaking came during Europe's phylloxera epidemic, a devastating pest that, beginning in the mid 1800's, ravaged thousands of hectares of Old World vineyards throughout the continent's winemaking regions. As a result, there were many experienced and respected European winemakers who, looking for work, came to the New World to capitalize on their expertise, and Chile was a prime beneficiary of this exodus.

However, the political instability in Chile during the late 20th century, land reforms under the Allende years, bureaucratic regulations, high taxes, and the isolation during the Pinochet regime, all combined to dampen growth in the Chilean wine industry. It was not until 1980 that restrictive domestic policies were repealed and the Chilean wine industry began to blossom again. Foreign investment re-entered the country, new winemaking techniques and technologies were introduced, and the country's wines came to be recognized on global markets. Equipment was updated, new drip irrigation systems were installed to replace the traditional flooding of fields, the ancient wooden vats were replaced with new stainless steel tanks as well as American and French oak barrels, and modern facilities were designed.

Importantly, some of the world's most prestigious names from the world of wine became involved in the country, with such brands as California's Mondavi, Miguel Torres, Kendall-Jackson, and France's Chateau Lafite Rothschild and Chateau Mouton Rothschild opening their own wineries in the country or collaborating with existing Chilean producers.

As an example, Casa Lapostolle, a winery located just south of Santiago, was founded by the Marnier family who created the famous orange scented French liqueur Grand Marnier in 1880 and the owners of Chateau Sancerre, one of France's most revered wineries. Lapostolle's 2001 Clos Apalta, a Bordeaux blend of three different grapes, was ranked as the number two wine in the world in 2004 by the Wine Spectator,

Today, Chile has become the world's tenth largest wine producing country and one of the largest exporters of wine to the United States, the

United Kingdom, Canada, Germany, Japan, and many other countries. In 2007 shipments of wine from Chile reached 592 million litres with a value well in excess of US $1 billion. Over the prior ten years, the industry has more than doubled, with approximately 62% of total production exported to more than 90 different countries. In 1995 there were only twelve wineries in Chile - now that number exceeds seventy, with 100,000 hectares of land under grape vines. Chilean wines have been honoured with top medals and awards at numerous prestigious international competitions around the world over the last twenty years.

To say that wine is important to Chile and Chileans is an understatement. Wine is consumed at both the daytime and evening meals, and is offered whenever a guest visits a Chilean home. The nationwide *Copec* fuel station chain will even give you a fine bottle of Mont Gras cabernet sauvignon with every oil change for your car. In Canada, we might receive a wine glass.

On one of our first trips to Chile, we were bundled into a truck by Pancho and Angela and driven south about an hour to the Cachapoal Valley to visit Vina Anakena and Vina Gracia.

Vina Anakena, started in 1998, has developed a number of superb *vino blanco* (white wine) varietals and is maturing a high quality *vino tinto* (red wine) portfolio from their Leyda and Ninquen vineyards. The winery exports its brands to thirty-two countries around the world. The Anekena name is derived from an Easter Island legend involving a precious seagull egg that was hidden in a hideaway, or *anakena,* on a distant offshore outcrop, Every year the bravest islanders swam the long distance to the island in search of the egg, and the one who carried it back was given the title of birdman, or *Tangata Manu.* All of Anakena's wine bottles are decorated with various symbols of ancient myths from Easter Island, a tribute to their country's history and tradition.

On our first visit to the winery, we were graciously hosted by owners Heather and Phillipe who showed us around and provided much insight into the founding and building of a winery in Chile. Anakena is also home to one of Pancho's major horse sculptures, painted a bright red and rising more than forty feet above the deep greens of the vineyard, accompanied by a plaque containing an ode to the Chilean horse that he had composed. It is a majestic sight.

Gracia de Chile, located nearby, saw its first grapes planted in 1989 with vineyards now located in most of Chile's important wine producing regions. The winery we visited was built in 1996 with a capacity of 9.5 million litres being aged in modern stainless steel tanks, as well as over 4,000 French oak barrels. The winery is owned by the Bodegas Corpora, one of Chile's wealthiest holding companies, who also own the *Explora* group of hotels, destination landmarks for those seeking adventure travel in the Atacama Desert, Patagonia or on Easter Island. The courtyard of Gracia is also home to a series of Pancho's magnificent stone sculptures that can be enjoyed by all visitors to the winery.

On our visit both wineries were holding harvest festivals with traditional Chilean music and other entertainment, delicious food, art exhibits, and, more importantly, sales of their recent vintages. Families were enjoying the warm day as their children ran about and danced to the music, while parents sampled the wines. Following numerous tastings, we acquired a few cases of top wines from each vineyard for, in Canadian wine buying terms, relatively little money for wines of such quality, character and depth. It was a wonderful day.

Despite the apparent success of these winery open-houses, wine tourism is just beginning to develop in Chile, and while most wineries do not permit visits, those that do often require advance reservations. These restrictions are loosening, with a number of wineries now welcoming visitors to their wine shops, tours and tasting rooms, as well as restaurants that rival any in the world.

One such location is Concha y Toro, Chile's largest producer and largest exporter, located in Pirque just down the road from Castillo Verde. Founded in 1883 by politician and businessman Don Melchor Concha y Toro, the winery was among the first to plant French Bordeaux grapes and import their own winemaker from France to nurture the vineyard and supervise the crafting of their wines. In 1933 the Company was listed on the Santiago Stock Exchange and then, in 1994, it became the world's first winery to list and trade on the New York Stock Exchange.

Concha y Toro produces what has become Chile's most prestigious cabernet sauvignon, Don Melchor, as well as the more popular wines under the Casillero del Diablo brand. Casillero del Diablo is named after a cave on the Pirque property that, legend has it, is home to the devil, who prevents the pilfering of wine from the vaults. Don Melchor stored his finest vintages in this ancient cellar, and used this legend to his advantage to protect his collection while he was absent on business trips.

We buy much of our wine from the beautiful Concha y Toro vineyard store, and have taken many guests to the winery to enjoy their guided tours and tastings. While the standard tour costs 6,000 pesos, or about Canadian $12, and includes two wine tastings, you can also book a much more extensive visit to the winery.

The *Don Melchor Tour*, costing approximately 85,000 pesos, or about US $170, provides you with a private tour of the winery that includes a visit inside the beautiful summer home of the Don Melchor family, built in 1885 but now used only for major events and banquets. Heads of State, and even the Pope, have dined in this fabulous hacienda.

More importantly, the *Don Melchor Tour* includes a special tasting in a private room with one of the company's winemakers. On our first encounter with this exclusive tour, we were fortunate to be hosted by José Manuel Garcia Huidobro, the Marketing Director for Conch y Toro. Sitting at a long table with eight to ten glasses of their best vintages in front of us, José Manuel walked us through the tastes and strengths of each wine, accompanied by small samples in a tapas format of local cheeses, meats, dried fruits and chocolates to accompany each wine. The tasting culminated with the sampling of three Don Melchor vintages, the winery's most celebrated and most expensive wines. A small glass of this exclusive brand costs about US $25 in the restaurant following the standard tour, but here you can sample a number of the brand's best years. The *Don Melchor Tour* is a lot of fun and very interesting, but don't plan on driving after the event.

Nearby is another well-respected winery, Vina Santa Rita, founded in 1880 by a well-respected politician and banker Domingo Fernandez Concha. Located in Alto Jahuel in the Maipo Valley, Santa Rita harvests premium grapes on approximately 1,000 hectares, as well as on land in most of Chile's other prime grape growing regions. It is the second largest land-owning winery in the country. After decades of family ownership, in 1980 the winery was purchased by Grupo Claro, a holding company that interestingly also owns the law firm we dealt with to purchase Castillo Verde.

The extensive Santa Rita property is home to La Casa de Dona Paula Restaurant, a National Monument where Dame Paula Jaraquemada once lived. During Chile's struggles to liberate the country from Spain in 1814, 120 of General Bernardo O'Higgins' soldiers and their horses found refuge in the cellar of the hacienda, now the restaurant, after a fierce battle in which they had been defeated in nearby Rancagua. When faced with the pursuing Spanish forces, Paula refused to let the Spanish invaders into her house and threw a brazier of hot coals at them. The Spanish left and O'Higgins, a hero of the liberation wars, was free to fight again.

Next to the restaurant is the Museo Andino, a well-respected museum opened in 2006 and home to the Claro family's extraordinary collection of pre-Columbian art and artifacts. Housed in a beautiful, light and open sandstone block building in the midst of native grass gardens, the extensive collection includes more than 1,800 Andean and Pre-Columbian archeological objects, pottery, ceremonial headpieces, silver Mapuche jewelry and items from the early history of Easter Island. Surrounded by beautiful views of the vineyards and the mountains, the collection is exquisitely displayed with descriptions in both Spanish and English. The galleries in the Museum are also used to host temporary art exhibits, and for three months included a retrospective of both Pancho's and Angela's sculpture and paintings.

Nearby is the Casa Real Hotel, a luxurious sixteen-room hotel situated in a 40 hectare park designed in 1882 by the French landscape architect Guillermo Renner and famed for having the largest bougainvillea in South America. Oddly, the hotel will not allow children as guests. We met a Canadian family travelling through Chile who had booked rooms at the hotel as part of their tour. Arriving late in the evening, they were informed their reservation could not be honoured as their ten-year old son was not allowed to stay in the hotel. They were told of other accommodation in the area, and luckily found rooms at a nearby French restaurant we frequent.

Chile is also home to what was thought to have been a lost grape, originally grown in the Bordeaux region of France. Carmanere, whose name originates with the Spanish word *carmine*, or crimson, fell prey to the dreaded phylloxera plague that ravaged most of France's vineyards late in the 19th century. While the other grapes that provided Bordeaux with its fame – cabernet sauvignon, cabernet franc, merlot, malbec and petit verdot – were revived by grafting vines onto roots resistant to the disease, the carmenere grape proved to be too fragile and became, so everyone thought, extinct.

Then, in 1994 a viticulturalist in Chile began checking the DNA at a number of merlot vineyards and found one type that differed slightly from its neighbours. Somehow, the long-lost carmanere grape had found its way to Chile from France more than 150 years earlier and had flourished in the country's dry, Mediterranean-like climate, mistakenly identified as merlot. Soon separated, carmanere has grown to become one of Chile's signature vintages, and a varietal that is growing in popularity around the world.

Among the top carmanere producing regions in Chile is the Colchagua Valley, about 90 minutes by car south of Santiago. Like all of the wine producing areas in Chile's central region, Colchagua benefits from its proximity to the Pacific Ocean to the west and the steep Andes Mountains rising to the east. The climate is dry with an annual average rainfall of only 38 millimeters, and the hot daytime temperatures are balanced by cool nights that are vital to maintaining the acidity levels in the region's grapes. The coastal mountain range that rises between Colchagua and the Pacific Ocean also creates a rain shadow that traps warm arid air in the valley, extending the growing season to create the necessary long and slow-ripening process that enhances the quality of its wines.

Colchagua is home to many of Chile's most respected vineyards, and is one of the most developed regions in terms of wine tourism with numerous opportunities to taste and buy their products and enjoy gourmet meals prepared with local produce. New boutique hotels are being developed, and one can spend many days leisurely sampling the fine wines, fabulous food and beautiful geography. There is even a "wine train", a resurrected track and ancient locomotive that on Saturdays conducts tours through the area, stopping at a number of wineries en route. Colchagua was one of our early introductions to the country's wines and wine regions, and we continually return to extend our explorations and knowledge of the area. The valley is also home to Roberto, Luis, and their eighty dogs.

CHAPTER SIXTEEN
LUIS AND ROBERTO

First introduced to us by Sergio and Marcela, Roberto and Luis live in Colchagua near the town of Perallilo in a true, authentic Chilean hacienda, called Santa Ana, that they are slowly restoring from what had largely been a ruin only ten years before. The property had been in Luis' family for generations until the land reforms under Salvador Allende caused the property to be divided among local farmers, also allowing them to live in the main house. Over the years, the numerous families who used the property watched as it fell into disrepair and, sadly, much of its original detailing and furniture were lost. Luis reclaimed the property by purchasing it back from the government, and since then has been on a mission to slowly restore the house to its previous grandeur.

Like most large Chilean haciendas, the house is built around a series of courtyards that are home to fountains, palms and other native trees, flower gardens, as well as sitting and dining areas. The rooms are all interconnected with doors that lead through each room into another, and all are open to the inner courtyards. There are three such courtyards at Santa Ana, with about ten rooms surrounding them. It is a bit of a maze, and easy to get lost after a long meal accompanied by the region's finest wines.

It is an amazing and beautiful property. Inside, the walls have been repaired and painted with murals done by Luis, an accomplished artist and photographer, while large statues, urns and other decorative pieces collected on the owners' travels through South America and Malaysia are carefully placed. Fireplaces are located in most rooms, as are comfortable chairs and couches. The property is tailor-made for entertaining, and Luis and Roberto spare no expense when guests arrive for dinner or the weekend.

They also own a lot of dogs, all of which resemble something like a miniature beagle or spaniel. All eighty have names, and all names are remembered. Many are allowed to live only in certain parts of the house, while most are contained in a lovely, large garden area with its own small brick cottage, complete with a fireplace, covered by a traditional terracotta tile roof. As the canine population has grown, a new sanctuary has been built in an adjoining field with fenced in runs and compact shelters. One guest referred to the compound as Guantanamo, although I am sure the lives these dogs live are far superior to the alternative of running the countryside as *quiltros*.

To accompany the eighty dogs and numerous guests visiting Roberto and Luis, there is also a ghost in the house. I was staying for a weekend with John, a lifelong friend from Canada, who was visiting Chile for the first time. We had enjoyed a simple but wonderful meal of pasta, salad and wine with Luis and two of his friends, one of whom was a renowned Chilean stage and television actress. We retired to our separate bedrooms quite late, and settled in for a good night's sleep.

Very early the next morning, the door handle to my room began to rattle and the panels to shake. Although the door was not locked, clearly someone was trying to get in. Then I heard what sounded like something heavy being dragged over the cobblestone and gravel courtyard outside my room. Mystified, I wondered what was going on, and then remembered that the other two guests were due to leave early that morning, and I was probably listening to their departure. I went back to sleep.

During breakfast later that morning, I mentioned that I was astonished to hear the guests leave so early given how much wine we had consumed the night before and the late hour we retired. Luis looked at me quizzically, saying that the guests had decided to leave the night before. My friend John had also heard the noises, and had come to the same conclusion. Luis then told us that we were the only people at the hacienda at that time, and we had probably heard the ghost. I have since learned that others have experienced the same sounds and rattling doors during the night.

Apparently sometime during the occupation of the property decades earlier a child had died and been buried just outside the wall of my bedroom. There were stories about how and why the child had passed away, but the truth has not been determined. The body had been exhumed a few years earlier during Roberto and Luis' reconstruction and placed in a proper cemetery. What we had heard, apparently, was the sound of this child trying to find something at Luis' hacienda, no one knows what. It is just another wonderful mystery in our Chilean adventure.

Driving in Colchagua, and indeed throughout Chile, you will see countless shrines on the side of the road, ranging from a small cross and a few rocks to large, elaborate structures with religious icons, candles, flags and personal effects. Called *animitas*, these shrines are constructed in memory of those who have lost their lives violently, such as in car accidents, avalanches, earthquakes and the like. The families who build these shrines believe that the soul, or *animita*, of the departed remains nearby, and is willing to intercede for the living with their God, the Virgin Mother, or whoever they pray to for good or better fortune.

On certain religious festivals or birthdays, relatives will gather at these shrines to commemorate the lives of the departed, and if the sheer number, size and the care taken to maintain many of these *animitas* is any indication, there is a widespread belief in the possibility of these intercessions. New Year's Eve appears to be an important date for families to visit the *animitas*, and you will see candles, coloured lights, and other types of decoration and illumination highlighting the owner's devotion everywhere you drive. Some are quite beautiful, and it is a solemn reminder of how one must take care, not only driving a car, but in all aspects of life.

Central to the Colchagua valley is Santa Cruz, a small but well established town that is the hub of the Valley's wine industry and a destination for wine lovers from around the world. Situated around a lovely town square, there is a small hotel and a number of restaurants and shops offering local crafts and fine meals. Each year in March the square also hosts the *Fiesta de la Vendimia*, or harvest festival, where one can sample the local vintages from most of the regions' fine wineries as well as traditional foods.

Just behind the town's central square is the *Museo de Colchagua*, one of the most comprehensive historical museums I have visited on my travels. It is the largest non-public museum in Chile, displaying a private collection of pre-Columbian art, paleontological specimens, fine Mapuche silver and gold jewelry, and many other items.

It is an extremely eclectic collection, and one wonders about the collecting habits of its founder. In addition to the types of historical exhibits one would expect to find at a regional museum, here you can also find: a large collection of ancient bugs preserved in amber (shades of Michael Crichton's movie Jurassic Park); Nazi memorabilia including uniforms, flags and even Herman Goering's pistol from the Second World War; an automobile collection that counts as its central attraction a Formula One racecar driven by Ayrton Senna, the celebrated Brazilian driver and triple Formula One Champion; an old railway train, complete with passenger cars and a reconstructed railway station; agricultural and wine making implements from many eras; and a wonderful collection of antique horse drawn carriages. Well organized and presented, the museum covers all periods of Chilean history, and contains something that will appeal to everyone.

However, some caution is needed if you take small children through the pre-Columbian art and ceramic exhibits. Many of the artifacts display the culture's fascination with fertility and sexuality, and a number of the vessels and sculptures include significant penile protuberances, pregnant women birthing, and numerous couples clearly enjoying one another in a rather carnal fashion and in a number of different positions. For the squeamish or the inhibited, one might consider missing these sections of the museum. I, however, thought they were most illuminating.

The museum was founded, constructed and is owned by a local businessman and philanthropist, who is also rumoured to be a former international arms dealer being sought to answer various criminal charges by a number of countries. He is a fugitive from the United States for selling arms to Saddam Hussein during the Iraq war, is supposed to have invented the deadly cluster bomb, and has been charged with laundering money and violating export laws. Unable to enter the United States or risk arrest, ironically much of his current wealth is being created through vineyard partnerships with California wineries and the export of Chilean wines to the US. He is married to a former top Chilean model, and while presently battling colon cancer, appears frequently in the Chilean social pages, a key area of interest in most national newspapers.

Another interesting sight to visit in the Colchagua Valley is *Casa el Huique*, one of the largest and best preserved old haciendas in Chile. Dating from 1828, the extensive buildings and grounds were the original center of the massive hacienda *San José del Carmen de el Huique*, farmland that extended at one time through most of the Colchagua Valley. The hacienda had been in the same Sánchez Errázuriz family for over 200 years, but was donated to the Chilean army in 1976 to prevent its destruction and to ensure its preservation and longevity. Today the hacienda and gardens are available to visitors, although it sometimes can be a bit challenging to find someone who will open the property for a tour.

The house and gardens contain a wonderful collection of period art and furniture, as well as many Errázuriz family heirlooms and photographs, including numerous reminders that one of *el Huique's* owners, Frederico Errázuriz Echaurren, served as President of Chile from 1896 to 1901. The hacienda is situated close to the Tinguirririca River (try saying this name out loud a few times to practice rolling your r's), and you can see on the interior walls the water line created when the river overflowed many years ago. Interestingly, our friend Pancho, Francisco Gazitua, is related to the Errázuriz family and had spent many summers at *el Huique*. He remembers fondly running through the hacienda's numerous courtyards and gardens as a child.

As you exit the Colchagua Valley to the west, you climb a series of steep hills through a predominantly pine forest that then meanders down to the coastal town of Pichilemu. Founded by Agustín Ross Edwards (there are those Chilean / English / Scottish names again) in 1885, the town was originally destined to become Chile's answer to the French Riviera with stately homes, fine hotels and a large casino. Using his government connections, Ross Edwards had obtained a casino license at the turn of the century and began construction of his showpiece entertainment palace. Unfortunately, he was outmaneuvered by more powerful and politically astute residents of Viña del Mar to the north and closer to Santiago, who lobbied and eventually were awarded Chile's exclusive right to operate casinos in 1932, and Pichilemu fell into a decline. As one wealthy lady from Santiago said to me, astonished that I would even consider visiting the town much less praise its interesting sights: "They should simply drop a bomb on the place so that it just goes away."

Today, Pichilemu has what many consider to be some of the finest surfing in South America. Although the Pacific waters are extremely cold, surfers from around the world flock to capture the left break at Punta de Lobos, a picturesque point of land that extends toward a large rock outcrop about six kilometers south of the town centre. Inside the break is a beautiful sandy beach where you can take surfing lessons or practice your technique before paddling out for the more challenging waves. Crowds of sea lions watch the surfers from the rocky cliffs, while surf fishermen cast into the waves for their dinners.

The land above and surrounding Punta de Lobos has recently been purchased by Jorge Lobo, an appropriately named entrepreneur and surfing addict hailing from Cuba. The son of a wealthy sugar family ousted from their homeland during the Castro revolution, Jorge and his brother, Mario, eventually arrived in Chile to participate in the country's growing prosperity. Mario is the managing Director for the famed Los Vascos winery in Colchagua, a partnership with the Rothschild family from France, while Jorge is taking his love of surfing to build a resort at what is one the world's best locations for the sport.

The fact that there are no real hotels or services to support tourism in this town is, to me, indicative of Chile's isolation, and its future potential. As one friend said after visiting Pichilemu with me: "Its like being in California during the 1960's". And he is right. There is a sense of wild optimism in the town and its people, although their ambitious plans are somewhat mitigated by a heartfelt desire to preserve the land, the environment, and the purity of the surfing culture. Jorge Lobo plans to construct a surfing resort on his land, but all of the buildings will be made of stone, only one or two storeys high, and nestled into the hillocks and dunes above the main surfing beaches. He told me that he plans to tailor his fees to a surfer's income, hoping that the well-off and the not-so-well-off surfing public will mingle together in the conjoined joy of the surfing life. I wish him the best of luck. And, despite some Chilean's desire to wipe the town off of the country's maps, Pichilemu is a beautiful place to visit and to partially re-live an alternative lifestyle that captured the imaginations of my generation in their youth.

CHAPTER SEVENTEEN
NERUDA'S GHOST

T he renovation and restoration of Castillo Verde was finally nearing completion in September 2007, almost fourteen months after we began the project. Despite the extended time taken, the numerous problems, interruptions, changes, additions and complicated decisions we had encountered, the finished property was everything we had dreamed it would be, and much more. It had been transformed from a house into a home, majestic yet comfortable, imposing yet proportionally correct.

The new entrance to the Castillo fit perfectly with the sprit of the house as huge wood planks, held together with large wrought iron brackets, are closed and secured inside with a hefty iron bar that hinges into a yoke to lock the portal, just like a traditional castle gate. Stone stairs encased in cast steel with a signature steel railing, all designed by Pancho and hand built by Humberto, wind up through the main hall to the second floor. All of the rooms are painted a deep white that perfectly sets off the blonde wood of the old plank floors and the new slate tiles downstairs. Above the new laundry room we discovered we could add another small bedroom off the guest suite, complete with a juliet balcony. It is perfect for friends visiting us with children. This room has been painted a deep red and is very cozy to rest, read, or simply gaze out at the garden.

As the project neared completion, we organized the shipment of our furniture, our extensive library, clothing, artwork, bicycles, skis, and many other belongings from Canada. Basically, when we sold our house in Canada to buy Castillo Verde, we put almost everything we owned into storage with an international mover who, when instructed, would pack the container and send it on its way across Canada, by ship to Valparaiso, then by truck to Santiago and finally to the Castillo. Included in the massive forty-foot shipping container were also the cabinets we had built in Canada for our new Chilean kitchen.

Before the furniture arrived, we wanted to spend one night in our almost-completed house. We purchased a mattress and box spring, set them up in our new bed room, and then wandered around the property in a little bit of shock at what we had accomplished. It came to me then that renovating a house must be a little bit like being pregnant. There is significant pain and discomfort during the pregnancy, and the term must always seem much longer than intended. And yet, when the baby is born, all thoughts of what was endured to produce the new child are forgotten. As we experienced for the first time the beautiful bedrooms, the majestic views, the comfortable living and dining areas, the potential of the gardens, we almost forgot what it had cost us in frustration, time and money to get there. At least, we almost forgot.

The first night was quite exciting. As the propane supply had not been fully inspected and therefore not connected to the house, we did not have any hot water. We then discovered that while the toilet in the turret bathroom worked, the sink did not – we had to use the washing-up facilities in another bathroom. A number of the new doors rattled quite noisily with the smallest gust of wind. We found spilled paint in a few areas, a number of plumbing details needed correcting, some lights did not work, and for the life of me I could not understand why a builder would forget that people needed to hang their towels in a bathroom.

To start the celebration we invited our caretaker Luis to join us for a glass of Chilean sparkling wine we had brought with us – Miguel Tores Pinot Noir Brut, the best available at the local grocery store in La Puntilla. To accompany the wine we enjoyed some fresh goat's cheese from a nearby agricultural college, along with prosciutto ham and bread from the adjacent farmer's market. As we did not have our kitchen cabinets or appliances installed, this would have to suffice as our first meal at Castillo Verde. During our quiet celebrations, we notice a condor, the national bird of Chile, hovering over the house and giving us a good look. Apparently, having a condor fly over you is a sign of good luck, and we certainly appreciated the majestic sight and the good fortune it portended for our future lives at Castillo Verde.

As our first evening wore on, we watched the sun slowly set into the hills and then bid Luis good night, about the only point of communication we could make given our rudimentary Spanish abilities, before climbing up our new stairs to the bedroom. It was only after turning out the lights that we heard the ghost of Neruda.

The Chilean hero Pablo Neruda, whose real name was Neftalí Ricardo Reyes Basoalto, is widely considered to be one of the most accomplished and influential poets of the twentieth century. He was awarded the Nobel Prize in 1971. In addition to his considerable contributions to the world of poetry and literature, Neruda also held a number of diplomatic posts and served as a senator for the Chilean Communist Party. He was forced into exile when Conservative President González Videla outlawed communism in September 1948, and for the next seven months he was hidden throughout the country by his supporters, smuggled from house to house often minutes away from arrest. In March 1949 he fled into Argentina by horseback, allegedly moving up the *Cajon del Maipo* and across the mountains to safety. His Nobel Prize acceptance speech recounts these adventures in some detail and with great drama. There are rumours that during his trek to Argentina he was housed in a small castle on the banks of the river Maipo, and, of course, Castillo Verde being the only castle in the area, we have adopted this myth to mean he stayed at our house.

In honour of this story, and as a house warming gift to us, Pancho made a beautiful weather vane to sit on top of the turret of Castillo Verde. He sculpted the vane out of forged steel to represent the fish symbol that is so often associated with Neruda's signature and identity. Approximately four feet long, it sits on a long pole seated carefully into a shoe that allows the vane to swivel in the wind. Unfortunately, the steel pole rubbing in the steel shoe made a loud moaning and groaning sound, moving through several octaves and intensity, all amplified greatly by the interior, cone-shaped dome of the turret located directly outside our bedroom. The sound was so loud, so eerie, and so haunting, that at first we thought we really did have a ghost living with us. When we discovered the true source of the phantasmagorical sounds, we naturally assumed it was the benevolent spirit of Chile's famous poet who had certainly visited and possibly once found sanctuary in Castillo Verde. Unfortunately, we found the ghost's sounds far too noisy for a restful sleep, and Pancho has since permanently welded the vane in a north south direction to represent the direction we have travelled from Canada.

Our son Jordan experienced the visit of a second ghost one night when he stayed alone in Castillo Verde. At the darkest hour he heard a rustling downstairs and a slow, methodical climbing up the stairs toward his bedroom. Clutching a knife under his pillow, he waited for the intruder to arrive. The door slowly opened.

Our neighbours next door, the Leteliers, have two golden retrievers, Cosmo and Emma. The male, Cosmo, had become quite enamoured with Jordan's female dog Daza, and visits her at every opportunity. Cosmo had also become quite adept at opening gates and doors, and somehow had managed to discover how to reach in to open the steel gate over our kitchen door, and then twist the door handle to open the door. As Jordan sat up abruptly and turned on his light to face the intruder, Cosmo blinked at him, wagged his tail, and gave a short bark of hello to Daza. Ever since we lock our doors and ensure the gate between Castillo Verde and Casa Blanca is firmly fastened.

As happy as we were with the maestros' efforts at Castillo Verde, we did have to go through one final adventure with our contractor, Rodrigo, as we conducted our final inspection in preparation for a sign off on his work. There were a few minor items he needed to rectify, which he agreed to complete in the coming days. He then handed me the final statement for his work.

The last time we had received an updated budget for the project the costs had climbed to 111 million pesos. Reasonable explanations had been presented, a detailed cost summary provided, and, although the anticipated final estimate was higher than we had anticipated, we were prepared. In reality, when we started the project we had assumed it would cost somewhere around US $200,000, and with this final estimate we were not far off.

But the final invoice added another 36 million pesos to the last estimate, about $75,000. We were dumfounded – how could the costs have escalated so much since what we had been told was the final estimate just a few weeks before? I stared at the piece of paper for a few moments, stuffed it in my pocket, and said I would be in touch.

What followed was a long and protracted negotiation. At first, I refused to pay, but recognizing that this escalation in costs was not something just pulled out of a hat, asked for a full accounting of all expenses incurred in the project. I received detailed work sheets for the time spent by each *maestro* as well as the amounts that had been paid for labour for each month of the project. Schedules of costs for all sub-contracted work, and lists of all the materials purchased were given to me. In an effort to explain what happened, I was even provided with how much profit Rodrigo's firm had made.

I then met with our architect Patricio, Rodrigo, and his financial partner. I presented my side of the issue, reviewing the time sheets and suggesting that, in reality, certain of the people had not really spent as much time on the project as was indicated in the worksheets. In addition, I claimed that they had taken at least two months longer to complete the work than they should have. We knew from others visiting the project on our behalf that many of the days we were not present on site, few of the *maestros* had turned up, unduly delaying the work. I offered, through my calculations, that by reducing this time that had been charged, as well as a few other disputed items, I would pay half the amount owing.

Rodrigo's partner, who spoke fluent English, then presented their case. He agreed that the project had taken much longer than it should, primarily due to the fact that Pirque was remote and many *maestros* would not travel that far. Others, who had agreed to be employed on the project, simply did not turn up for work as they had found other jobs closer to home. Thus the length of time taken to complete the project was not due to management issues but in reality the inability to obtain sufficient *maestros* on a consistent basis to perform the necessary work.

The second issue we were told was the fact that, in Chile, hardly anyone renovates old houses. The typical project was to tear down anything old and replace it with a totally new, more modern structure. Thus, many of the tasks they had to perform were unusual for the *maestros* employed, and it would have been much simpler and less costly to have built a new house.

I wondered aloud why we had not been informed of these issues at the outset? If we had known the project would cost significantly more than double the amount in the original estimate, we might have made some different decisions. Rodrigo's partner agreed, and as a gesture to settle the final amount owing, offered that the bulk of Rodrigo's profit on the project would be forfeited, reducing the amount owing to approximately 25 million pesos. We agreed, as long as the outstanding amount could be settled with twelve monthly cheques and no interest and financing charges assessed. We had a deal, and we were done.

At long last, our furniture arrived from Canada soon after the contractors finally departed. A massive forty-foot long shipping container was delivered to the Castillo, along with an army of professional movers who unloaded, unwrapped and positioned all of our belongings, including our extensive library, clothing, couches, chairs, tables, artwork and the new kitchen cabinets we had obtained in Canada. Once placed in their new rooms, everything looked like it belonged and had been there for years. The appliances were delivered, surprisingly on time and with everything accounted for, and we spent our first weeks getting everything sorted, installed, set-up and to our liking, adjusting and fine tuning as we became more comfortable and lived in our new house. Trips to local home centres, department stores and other suppliers became a daily occurrence as we added the final touches to the various rooms. Humberto was kept very busy correcting the deficiencies from the original work as toilets needed proper seating, some light switches operated incorrectly, taps required installation, and many other tasks. He was, and remains, an invaluable member of our new family. Meanwhile, Maria kept us fed with her wonderful cooking, and, yes, her empanadas are exquisite.

CHAPTER EIGHTEEN

WHAT WILL THE FUTURE BRING?

171

Our first protracted stay in Castillo Verde lasted just over six weeks, from early December 2007, through Christmas and New Years, and into the first two weeks of 2008. We experienced our first warm, non-snow related Christmas with our children, and it was a wonderful holiday season. Friends arrived at different times to visit us, and everything in the house worked reasonably well, save for a few frustrating sessions with the hot water system that was rectified with the installation of a new boiler.

The weather could not have been better – it did not rain for the entire period we were in Chile. The mornings dawned with bright sun, temperatures warming up through the day to the high 20 degree centigrade range, tempered by a constant and refreshing breeze from the mountains, and then cooling off into the mid-teens during the night for a wonderful and restful sleep. We watched the Maipo River as, swollen and loud from the rapid spring and summer snow melt in the Andes in early December, it gradually fell to a more sedate level producing a background sound that was as peaceful as it was exotic.

On the day we were returning to the snow and cold of a Canadian January, I sat in a chair in our bedroom to put socks and leather shoes on my feet for the first time in almost two months. As I leaned over to tie up my shoes, I wondered what the future would bring for us in our new home. What did I want Castillo Verde to be as our lives expanded in Chile?

I recalled a visit with one friend in Canada during the time we were debating with ourselves whether or not we should proceed with the purchase of Castillo Verde. Our businesses in Canada were both booming, we were comfortable with our standard of life, we were getting a bit older, and the thought of owning and renovating a property so far away, and the debt load resembling most developed nations that we would be taking on was becoming increasingly daunting, especially as we struggled with *uso fructo*, water rights, different currencies, the Spanish language, and all things foreign lurking in Chilean culture and history.

Our friend pulled a tape measure out of his pocket and, extending the tape to the ground to measure 84 inches, indicated that this was the average life span of the typical Canadian male. He then pointed to my age on this scale, clearly and irrevocably showing me how much of my life was behind me, and how little, in relative terms, was remaining.

"Do you want to spend these last few inches being safe, reducing risk, taking the conventional route, being normal?" he asked. The answer was immediately self-evident, and from that point forward we decided that Castillo Verde, and some part of a life in Chile, was firmly in our future.

As I sat back in the chair that day, the leather shoes tied, the bags packed for the return to Canada, I mused on what might be in this future.

Certainly, spending time in Chile would keep my mind active, especially as we worked on becoming familiar with the local language. They say that as you get older, learning another language becomes increasingly difficult, and I knew that the struggle would keep me mentally challenged for years to come. I believe the mind is like a muscle and needs regular exercise to keep it fit. My efforts to learn Spanish, to think in Spanish, would be an epic journey that would keep me mentally engaged well into my dotage.

And learning Spanish is a key priority. One of the most frustrating aspects of our three years buying and renovating Castillo Verde has been our inability to properly communicate and interact with those around us. Few Chileans speak English, and because everything we needed to accomplish over those three years had been so critical to do properly, we always had someone with us who could translate and keep our best interests at the forefront of all negotiations and decisions. While I believe we did do everything properly and legally sound, and I am surprised at how much Spanish we did pick up in our daily struggles to be understood, I missed learning more about the people we came into contact with, not hearing their stories first hand, understanding their family backgrounds, and, more importantly, what it is like to live in Chile. Because a country is its people, and over the last three years we had not really gained much real insight into the history, culture and spirit that form the backbone of this long and varied land. I look forward with great excitement to capturing these nuances and the understanding and meaning that only deep conversation can bring.

It will also be very interesting to experience how it is to live in a foreign country, to be an immigrant, a stranger in a strange land. As a sixth-generation Canadian, and before this adventure began, I used to scoff at people who spoke English improperly, who did not understand the customs of our country, who did not seem to fit in. Now I know what it is like to not be able to communicate, and when I try to speak Spanish, to see the beginnings of a smile, or worse, the confusion as to what I was trying to say. I now know how to ask for and pay a restaurant bill in Chile, what they mean when they show you the register on the pump at a gas station, why it takes three or four different people to purchase an item in a store. I also have a much greater understanding and respect for the effort it takes to be an immigrant, and how difficult is the struggle to make sense of everything around you. Clearly the rest of the world is not like Canada, and I am excited and a bit apprehensive about celebrating these differences.

I look forward to deepening the relationships with our new Chilean friends, and meeting more of the wonderful people who make up this country. It is difficult to convey how helpful and how supportive everyone has been as we progressed through the steps necessary to buy and renovate Castillo Verde. I am not sure we would have been able to get things done without the kind assistance of Pancho and Angela, the entire Letelier family, Humberto and Maria, our muse Haydee, Michael Dyson across the street, Andres our lawyer, David our banker, and so many others. We have also been warmly welcomed into so many homes that reciprocating this wonderful hospitality will take us forever.

I am also excited about the opportunity to explore this country, and indeed all of South America, more extensively. Another unfortunate aspect of our three year effort to own and transform Castillo Verde was our inability to travel very far from the property. We did manage a few trips with friends a bit south and north, but we have only dented the fantastic sites and cultural experiences this vast country and continent can offer. From the northern deserts through the southern Lake District to the majesty of Patagonia and Antarctica, all of Chile awaits us. The architecture, night life and tango of Buenos Aries is only a short flight from Santiago, as are the ancient ruins of Machu Pichu, the mysterious cairns of Easter Island, Brazil's Anteplana and many other historic sites. There is also the opportunity to re-awaken my love of skiing and enjoy the spectacular mountains during the Northern summer months. We can resurrect our fly fishing gear and visit some of the best trout and salmon rivers in the world. Chile is a bicycling nation, and I look forward to getting back in the saddle to slowly explore the countryside around Castillo Verde and the Maipo canyon. All of this, and more, will be a part of our future.

Chile will also be a refuge from the harsh Canadian winter. Karen suffers from arthritis, and the warm, dry Chilean climate works wonders to reduce her pain and provide her with more mobility. As we age and become less able to adapt to the cold and snow of the north, Castillo Verde will provide us with a much healthier climate and environment in which to live.

Another exciting endeavor will be our garden. In total, we now have almost 2.5 acres of land on which we can imprint our gardening ambitions. A vast number of new and beautiful Chilean flora await our exploration, and we look forward to reading and learning about the native flowers, trees, shrubs and grasses, visiting the numerous *viveros*, or nurseries, that surround us, and watching as our garden grows and develops. And knowing Karen, I recognize that the garden will never be complete.

But most importantly, Castillo Verde will be a place our family and friends can come together and join us in this huge adventure. Already our daughter Sarah and her surfing boyfriend have discovered the attractions of the left break off Punta de Lobos near Pichilemu. Our eldest son Ben has visited with a number of his close friends, all of whom want to return to enjoy the peace and tranquility of Pirque, as well as continue sampling the exciting nightlife in Santiago and Valparaiso. And now our youngest son Jordan is living full time in Chile, has become completely bilingual, and is investigating the huge opportunities open to him to create a new life in this very young country.

So as I finish tying my shoes and prepare to leave for the airport, I wonder if the time, effort and money it took to buy Castillo Verde will be counted as the best, or the worst decision we have made in our lives. Somehow, I am confident the future will prove it to be the best.